singletrack ANTHOLOGY
Central Oregon

Get Lost.

The legendary performance goes off-road. Porsche has once again elevated the harmony of man and machine with a new breed of mountain bike. The Porsche of mountain bikes. Premium components and forward-thinking designs mesh to help you master the roads less traveled. And lose yourself in adventures for which there is no substitute.

Carrera Motors of Bend. Come by and see what we're all about.

1-800-842-1584 or blaze a trail to www.carreramotors.com.

PORSCHE

Bike Evolution

Bike FS

Bike S

Porsche now starting at $2100.

Come into Carrera Motors of Bend for a thorough test drive of the latest edition to the Porsche family. Mention this ad and receive $100 off the manufacturers suggested price. It's that easy.

Carrera Motors, Inc.,
1045 S.E. Third Street, Bend, Oregon 97702
541/382.1711 **800.842.1584**
www.carreramotors.com

First Published April 1998 by
Hood River Publishing Company ©
P.O. Box 353, Hood River
Oregon 97031, USA

Creation modification of all maps, graphic design elements and
devices, text, illustrations, pictograms, and etcetera
© copyright Hood River Publishing Company 1998.

Direction, Design and Pre-Press Production by Tyler Barnes
Digital Imaging by Wilson Enterprises, Hood River, Oregon
Repro by Bruno at Mill Cross Litho, Portland, Oregon
Binding by Northwest Bindery, Portland, Oregon
This is a 100% Oregon Product.

The representation in this guide is no proof of an existence of
a right of way, trail, road, highway or route. The representation of any and all specifically marked trails, paths, or roads
does not necessarily guarantee their existence.

Mountain biking is a dangerous sport. Hood River Publishing
Company, the authors or any of their affiliates take no
responsibility for loss of job, spouse, life or limb as a result of
using this or any other Hood River Publishing Company
product. That said ... Enjoy.

ISBN 0-9663288-0-9

photo (this page) — Bob Woodward
cover photo — Deschutes Historical Society
back cover photo — Bob Woodward

singletrack ANTHOLOGY
Central Oregon

SPECIAL THANKS

We owe a debt of gratitude to many people. Michael Heidenreich for the gracious hospitality, Brad Boyd (Eurosports) for sharing his wealth of knowledge, Don and Susan (Sunnyside Sports) for their recommendations, Mike and Eric (Hutch's) for pointing us the right way, mayor Bob Woodward (photos) for capturing the essence of Central Oregon, Tom Fallen and Rob Cunningham (Bike Gear Intl.) for wrenching on the Porsches, Steve Hayden (Deschutes National Forest) for verifying our info, Jen Hill (KTVZ-21) for reliable Central Oregon weather forecasts, Rodney Renbarger I for his keen design eyes, Susie for feeding the dogs, Jenifer Colman for helping with the huge task of editing, Aletta Wilson for additional editing, and Heather Ferris for her friendship, support and guidance. Everyone else who helped make this guidebook possible ... you know who you are. Thank you.

Please support the people and businesses who promote mountain biking in Oregon.

Special thanks to Porsche Mountain Bikes of North America, and Neil Bishop and Sunny Hisel, at Carrera Motors of Bend, for realizing the value of our product and theirs.

PORSCHE
MOUNTAIN BIKES

Carrera
MOTORS
BEND, OR

Oregon's Biggest Mountain is Our Back Yard.

MT. HOOD SKIBOWL MOUNTAIN BIKE PARK

The Northwest's longest established lift assisted mountain bike park.

2 to 3 lifts serving 45 miles of signed and maintained mountain bike trails from Memorial Day thru October.

Slope side mountain bike rentals and service. Front and Full Suspension Demos.

Site of NORBA Oregon State Championship Series mountain bike races.

Guided tours for groups of any size. Ranging from an easy cruise with lakeside picnic to leg burning and tooth rattling singletrack loops.

Mountain bike lessons for all abilities from local pros Wednesdays thru Sundays.

Bike maintenance clinics slope side at the Hurricane Shop from authorized technicians.

MT. HOOD SKIBOWL SUMMER ACTION PARK!
(Where You're in Control)

Featuring more than 26 attractions. Apline Slide, Free-fall Bungee, Rapid Riser, Indy and Kiddie Carts, Batting Cages, Power Skateboards, horse and pony rides, Scenic Sky/Mountain Bike Chair rides, Kid's Play Park, Adventure River Ride, mini and Frisbee golf, nature interpretive hikes plus a lot more!

☐ **FREE TRAIL PERMIT.**

Bring this guidebook with you to Mt. Hood Skibowl and get your first trail permit absolutely FREE!

View of Mt. Hood Skibowl base area 1600' below from atop Skibowl Peak, access via Lower Bowl and Upper Bowl chairlift with a 95% singletrack descent. Mt. Hood and mountain biker photos by Randy Hopfer.

MT. HOOD SKIBOWL Mt. Bike Racing

Action Park 503/222-BOWL (2695) or 800-SKIBOWL

Bike Shop 503/272-3206 ext.244

Race Info Line 503/272-0146

Lodging and Camping info call toll free 888/622-4822

www.skibowl.com

Contents

Bend 12-34

Sisters 36-48

Sunriver 50-60

Top Swampy Lakes Trail. **photo:** Bob Woodward
Middle McKenzie River Trail. **photo:** Tyler Barnes
Bottom Deschutes River Trail. **photo:** Bob Woodward

Sleek.

ENDORPHIN
sugg.retail
$32.00

Functional.

PHLYSWATER
sugg.retail
$28.00

Affordable.

NITE CRAWLER
sugg.retail
$32.00

Field Tested by The Anthologists.

The Central Oregon Trail Alliance (COTA) is a non-profit, volunteer based organization founded to promote responsible trail use, to prevent trail closures and to maintain unpaved multiuse and singletrack trails for bicycling in the Central Oregon area. COTA seeks to promote trail bicycle opportunities through stewardship, environmental and social responsibility, education and a spirit of cooperation among all trail users and land management agencies. COTA collaborates with the US Forest Service, Bureau of Land Management and other public land agencies. Together we advocate the following programs:

Trail Stewardship

A program to monitor, report on, and maintain trails and trail signs through volunteer efforts and funding.

Cycling Education

A program to teach cyclists safe, low impact cycling techniques that emphasize safety and courtesy toward other trail users and environmental sensitivity.

Trail Days

An opportunity to participate in improving existing trails and building new ones when appropriate in collaboration with the US Forest Service and other land management agencies.

COTA Member benefits

Your annual membership fee will be used to help maintain our trails, maintain access for all trail users, promote safe and responsible riding in Central Oregon. Your membership also entitles you to the following benefits ...

Bike Shop Discounts

Receive discounts and other special COTA Member benefits from participating local bike shops.

The Rider / Trail Network

Through COTA you can discover new trails to ride and meet new people to ride with. This is also available to anyone who attends a COTA activity.

COTA Hotline 541/385-1985

COTA Membership Form

COTA
CENTRAL OREGON TRAIL ALLIANCE
Where The Trail Ends Is Up To You

Name _____

Address _____

City _____ St _____ Zip _____

phone (hm) _____

Phone (wk) _____

❏ Yes, I would like to volunteer for trail maintenance.

❏ Yes, I would like to attend trail access/government meetings.

❏ Yes, I would like to help with the education program.

❏ Yes, I would like to volunteer my services. Please call me.

Please complete this form and send your $10 membership fee to

COTA, 1293 NW Wall #72, Bend, Oregon 97701.

Please don't mail cash. Makes checks payable to COTA.

FOR MORE INFO CALL (541)385-1985

copy this Membership Form or send a separate piece of paper with your info

For the cost of an innertube and tire irons you can make a positive impact on the quality of Central Oregon's trails, and our environment.

This space was provided to COTA free of charge in an effort to help boost membership and trail awareness. All cyclists who enjoy mountain biking in Central Oregon need to join COTA.

Using the Guide.

The Singletrack Anthology guidebooks are written with all ability levels in mind. Our goal is to keep the guidebook simple and easy to read using a rating system based on the universal codes seen at ski resorts around the world. Key information for each trail is placed in the same location on a full-page spread, creating a consistent layout for every ride.

Key to Symbols.

Familiarizing yourself with the symbols and nomenclature used throughout the book will help in reading and understanding its contents.

A. Junction point on the map with letter corresponding to navigation chart sidebar.

Green: Easier trail section.

Blue: More difficult trail section.

Black: Most difficult trail section.

Alternative trail/route (not rated).

1.7 Mileage distance between junctions.

Closed to bicycles.

Rim Trail 57   Common Forest Service trail name.

RD300   USDA Forest Service numbered roads.

Services as indicated:
Food, drinking water, restrooms,
phone, information, ranger station.

Established campsite

Shelter

Boat ramp

Using Common Sense.

MOUNTAIN BIKING IS HAZARDOUS.

This guidebook is not a substitute for common sense and good judgement nor is it a substitute for other topographical maps and route finding skills. Know your own limits and the limits of those in your party. Once you are on the trail you are along way from professional aid and medical assistance. You are going into the wilderness where conditions are variable and can change rapidly.

Using Tools ... and Bringing Them.

Tools are an indispensable item to carry. Knowing how to use them is even more important. Carry a patch kit, tire irons and know how to change a flat. Other recommended tools include a chain tool, an allen wrench set, a small screwdriver, money, matches, rain gear and imagination. Unless you are Meriwether Lewis, and excellent at judging distance, we recommend a calibrated odometer for checking your mileage.

www.SingletrackAnthology.com

This corresponding website provides registered users with the most current information on the trails described in the Central Oregon edition, plus local weather, trail issues and advocacy as well as information on current and future books. Registration is FREE with your book purchase and entitles users to on-line updates, bonus rides, and an on-line forum to discuss and share your singletrack experiences, give us feedback and let fellow cyclists know of other fun rides in your area.

The Left Page.

How difficult is the ride? How do I get there? How much climbing is there? How long is it? What should I expect on the trail? Everything you need to choose the best ride for you and your party is here.

The Right Page.

Which way do I go? How difficult is the actual section of the trail ahead? Where am I? Nearly everything you need to navigate the trail is on this page. Although other maps are useful depending on the ride.

Quick Info at Top...
Users, terrain, fitness, seasons, popularity.

Getting There...
Directions with distance to the trailhead.

On the Trail...
Highlights of the ride, what to expect, general description.

Notes... Other info.

Elevation Profile...
Depiction of elevation gain/loss of ride.

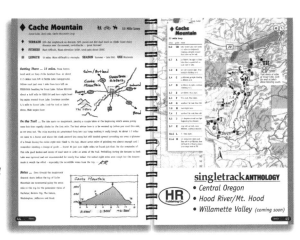

Trail Map...
Topographical map based on USDA Forest Service "Fire Maps" with trail, distances, junction points and related services depicted.

Navigation Bar...
Junction points as depicted on map with directional info, key junctions and other navigational clues.

Trail Page Sponsor...
who supports mountain biking in Oregon.

Rating the Rides.

Each trail has an overall rating based on Terrain, Fitness and Length as described below.

TERRAIN

● *easier* – firm singletrack surface, dirt or gravel dual track, paved roads or trails, overall less technical.

■ *more difficult* – higher % of singletrack, higher % technical conditions, some mild exposure.

◆ *most difficult* – highest % of singletrack, highest % of technical surface conditions with rocks, roots, water crossings, exposure.

FITNESS
*see elevation profiles

● *easier* – lower elevations, shorter total gain.

■ *more difficult* – 2500' to 4500' mean elevation, moderate gain.

◆ *most difficult* – over 4500' mean elevation, longer climbs with the most total elevation gains.

LENGTH
and navigation skills

● *easier* – 8 miles or less. Easier to navigate, trail well marked.

■ *more difficult* – 8 to 20 miles. Easier to more difficult to navigate.

◆ *most difficult* – more than 20 miles. Solid navigation skills required.

Bend
Oregon

top — Mike Heidenreich and Kent descending from Swede Ridge (p.22). **photo** Tyler Barnes
above — Tumalo Falls at North Fork Trailhead ... circa 1993 (p.26). **photo** Bob Woodward
opposite — Aspen glades in Shevlin Park (p.14). **photo** Bob Woodward

Shevlin Park

Shevlin Park Loop – City of Bend Parks

🚶🚶 🚲 **4.5 Mile Loop**

- **TERRAIN** 85% singletrack with 15% dual track. Some rocky trail sections, mild exposure with short technical descents, dusty summer conditions.

- **FITNESS** Easier ride, shorter in length, mean elevation 3700', total elevation gain about 320'.

- **LENGTH** 4.5 miles. Easier to navigate. **SEASON** Year Round*. **USE** Heavy.

  *winter weather permitting

Getting There ... 4 miles. From Bend, head west for Shevlin Park Road from downtown on either Newport or Galveston Avenue. We stopped by the Newport Market, on Newport Ave., for Clifbars and aprés ride refreshments. Once past 14th street, westbound on Newport, it shortly becomes Shevlin Park Road. Look for Shevlin Park just over 4 miles from downtown Bend on your left. Ride begins here.

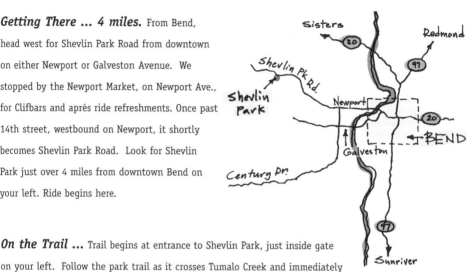

On the Trail ... Trail begins at entrance to Shevlin Park, just inside gate on your left. Follow the park trail as it crosses Tumalo Creek and immediately climbs to a plateau above the Creek. We just stayed on the beaten path as it followed both dual track and singletrack sections. At about the halfway mark we descended back down to Tumalo Creek. Watch out in this section as the descent is tricky - hey ... even I walked my bike. After crossing Tumalo Creek on a narrow bridge, look for the trail as it climbs a singletrack back up onto the ridge to the west. I found the return on the opposite ridge really fun with rolling terrain and gentle curves on the trail. Along the ride, several other trail options exist, but we just followed the busiest looking trail sections. Keep in mind this is a very popular area for hikers, runners, picnickers and other cyclists, so please ride carefully, under control and expect to see other park users. — *T.B.*

Notes ... Even though Shevlin Park is classified as an overall easier ride the terrain is rated more difficult. Exercise caution on all the descents as loose rock and dust can make them very challenging for about any cyclist.

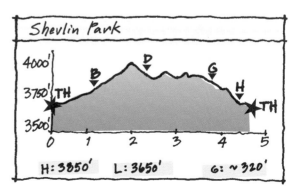

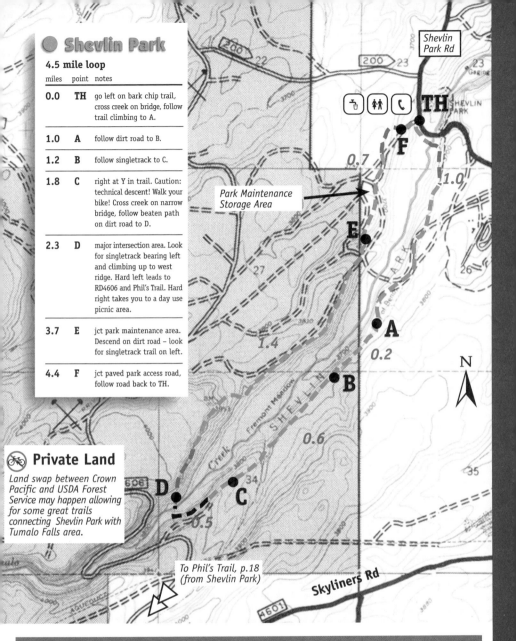

● Shevlin Park

4.5 mile loop

miles	point	notes
0.0	TH	go left on bark chip trail, cross creek on bridge, follow trail climbing to A.
1.0	A	follow dirt road to B.
1.2	B	follow singletrack to C.
1.8	C	right at Y in trail. Caution: technical descent! Walk your bike! Cross creek on narrow bridge, follow beaten path on dirt road to D.
2.3	D	major intersection area. Look for singletrack bearing left and climbing up to west ridge. Hard left leads to RD4606 and Phil's Trail. Hard right takes you to a day use picnic area.
3.7	E	jct park maintenance area. Descend on dirt road – look for singletrack trail on left.
4.4	F	jct paved park access road, follow road back to TH.

Shevlin Park Rd

Park Maintenance Storage Area

● Private Land

Land swap between Crown Pacific and USDA Forest Service may happen allowing for some great trails connecting Shevlin Park with Tumalo Falls area.

To Phil's Trail, p.18 (from Shevlin Park)

Skyliners Rd

Swampy Lakes

🚶🚶 🚴 🏇 **4 Mile Loop**

Swampy Lakes Loop from Swampy Lakes Sno Park

TERRAIN 90% dirt singletrack, 10% dual track, seasonal sandy conditions, some tricky rocky and rooted trail sections.

FITNESS Easier ride, shorter in length. Mean elevation 5800', total gain about 250'.

LENGTH 4.2 miles. Easier to navigate.   **SEASON** Summer – Fall.   **USE** Moderate.

Getting There ... 16 miles. From Bend head out of town on Cascade Lakes Highway, RD 46, toward Mt. Bachelor for about 16 miles. Take a right into the Swampy Lakes SnoPark and look for the trailhead on the north end of the parking area. Although restrooms are available at the trailhead there is no drinking water, so fill your water bottles in town.

On the Trail ... This shorter loop ride is great for beginning mountain bikers at just over 4 miles of trail, offering cooler, high alpine forest riding conditions. Expect seasonal sandy trail conditions, tricky rooted and rocky sections as well as buffed out, smooth cruising singletrack. Along the ride numerous winter recreation trails exist, however the main trail is fairly easy to follow. The Swampy Lakes Shelter, at about the half-way point, serves as a good spot to rest. During the ride I couldn't help but imagine the mid-winter scene of tree bows drooping heavy with snow and the smell and sound of a crackling fire in the Swampy Shelter stove, offering refuge from a cold Central Oregon winter. But hey ... its summer and mountain biking season. From the shelter, Kent and I continued heading around the Swampy Lakes to the right on more singletrack, then picked up a dual track returning us to the Swampy Lakes Sno Park. This is a definite "must ride" for anyone looking for a fun beginner trail in the area. — *T.B*

Notes ... "The Swampy Lakes are really more like swamps and make perfect breeding habitat for mosquitoes," — Steve Hayden, Deschutes National Forest. We must have hit it well after the hatch ... not a single pesky bite although you may want to bring some repellent just in case.

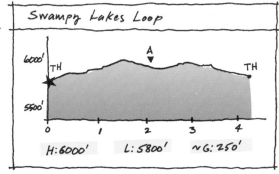

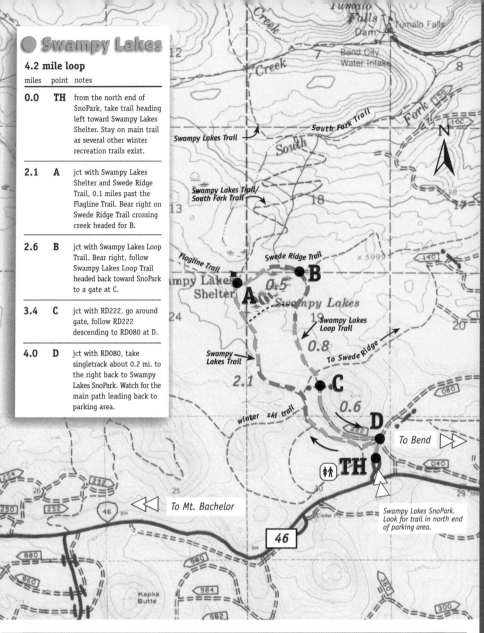

Swampy Lakes

4.2 mile loop

miles	point	notes
0.0	TH	from the north end of SnoPark, take trail heading left toward Swampy Lakes Shelter. Stay on main trail as several other winter recreation trails exist.
2.1	A	jct with Swampy Lakes Shelter and Swede Ridge Trail, 0.1 miles past the Flagline Trail. Bear right on Swede Ridge Trail crossing creek headed for B.
2.6	B	jct with Swampy Lakes Loop Trail. Bear right, follow Swampy Lakes Loop Trail headed back toward SnoPark to a gate at C.
3.4	C	jct with RD222, go around gate, follow RD222 descending to RD080 at D.
4.0	D	jct with RD080, take singletrack about 0.2 mi. to the right back to Swampy Lakes SnoPark. Watch for the main path leading back to parking area.

To Bend

To Mt. Bachelor

Swampy Lakes SnoPark. Look for trail in north end of parking area.

The famous local ride including Jim's Trail, Kent's Trail and Paul's Trail.

■ **TERRAIN** 60% singletrack, 40% dual track, seasonal dusty conditions, some technical sections.

■ **FITNESS** More difficult, moderate in length. Mean elevation 4000', total gain about 1000'.

■ **LENGTH** 16 miles. More difficult to navigate. **SEASON** Spring – Fall. **USE** Heavy.

Getting There ... 3 miles. Ride or drive ... you decide. From Bend's westside, go west on Galveston straight past 4-way stop at 14th street. Galveston becomes Skyliners Road and at just over 2 miles, look for paved RD220 on your left. Go left and follow RD220 about a half mile to jct with RD4606, a red cinder road, and trailhead marker. Ride begins here.

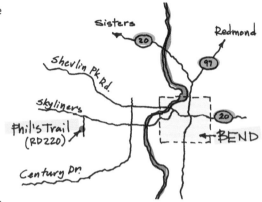

On the Trail ... "This is a must-do ride for anyone looking for a local's riding spot," according to Eric at Hutch's Bike Shop – we agree. Phil's Trail is one of the closest singletrack rides to town starting just three miles from Bend's popular westside, sandwiched between Skyliners Road and Century Drive. Phil's Trail starts off as abandoned dual track roads then quickly becomes the singletrack fun Phil intended, winding through second growth pine and thick manzanita. Keep on your toes because chances are you'll be sharing the trail with some speedy chipmunks. Bear in mind several spur roads and trails exist taking different routes to Kent's Trail, Ben's Trail and So-and-so's Trail ... you get the idea, however the main trail, Rt#24.5, seems to be fairly well marked with brown bicycle route signage. In general, if climbing you are probably heading west toward Mt. Bachelor and if descending you are heading east toward town. Regardless of direction, most of the trails are between Skyliners Road and Century Drive, so if you get turned around, as we did, you will probably find your way back to the trailhead. Oh, and if you see Phil, Jim or Paul be sure to thank 'em. — *T.B*

Notes ... Due to the ever changing trail system in the area keep a look out for the beaten path, trust your instincts and above all have a great ride! There are logging operations scheduled for the Fall of 1999 so check locally for updated info or on our web site at www.SingletrackAnthology.com.

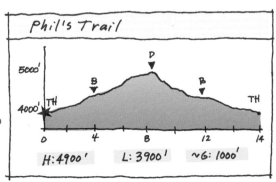

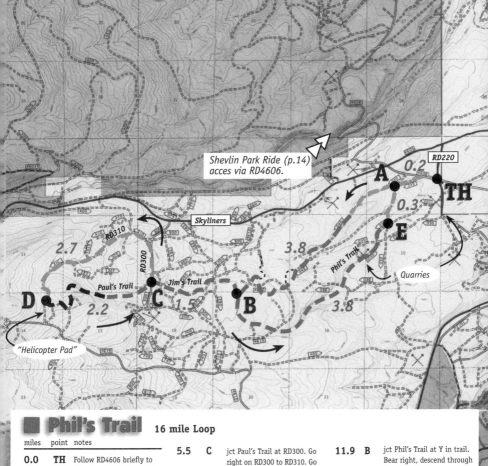

Shevlin Park Ride (p.14) acces via RD4606.

RD220

A 0.2

TH

0.3

E

Skyliners

RD310

RD300

2.7

3.8

Phil's Trail

Quarries

Paul's Trail

Jim's Trail

D

2.2

C 1.5

B

3.8

"Helicopter Pad"

Phil's Trail   16 mile Loop

miles	point	notes
0.0	TH	Follow RD4606 briefly to abandoned RD049 on left.
0.2	A	jct Phil's Trail Rt#24.5. Follow RD049 and bike signage around a dirt mound. Return trail is on the left from E, stay straight headed for B.
4.0	B	jct Y in trail just past RD4610. Stay straight, now on Jim's Trail, but still Rt#24.5 to C.
5.5	C	jct Paul's Trail at RD300. Go right on RD300 to RD310. Go left on RD310 climbing to D, still on Rt#24.5.
8.2	D	jct top of Paul's Trail near "Helicopter Pad", look for singletrack descending to C. Caution: technical descent.
10.4	C	jct RD300 at C completing a loop. Follow Jim's Trail again, descending to B.
11.9	B	jct Phil's Trail at Y in trail. Bear right, descend through dry canyon. At quarry, trail follows dual track RD030, then RD020 to E.
15.7	E	jct narrow dual track off of RD020. Look for bike signage and beaten path on the left heading for A.
16.0	A	jct A again. Go right to TH completing the loop.

Deschutes River Trail

From Meadow Picnic Area to Benham Falls and Sunriver

21 Mile O&B

- **TRAIL**   85% singletrack, 15% dual track, mild exposure, mostly smooth trail, some technical sections, very scenic.

- **FITNESS**   More difficult. Mean elevation 4000', total gain about 700'.

- **LENGTH**   21 miles. Easier to navigate.   **SEASON** Spring – Fall.   **USE** Extreme.

Getting There ... 6 miles. From Bend head west out of town on Cascades Lakes Highway, RD46, past Mt. Bachelor Village and Entrada Lodge to gravel RD100 on your left. Go left on RD100 as it skirts the edge of a golf course then descends to the Deschutes River's edge to Meadow Camp Picnic/Day Use Area. Look for trailhead signs for the Deschutes River Trail, Rt#2.3. Ride begins here.

On the Trail ... The 10 plus miles of scenic singletrack between the Meadow Camp Picnic/Day Use Area and Sunriver are popular with everyone. The singletrack trail follows the Deschutes River as its waters cascade over Benham Falls and through Lava Island Falls as well as other areas of rapids. You are likely to see whitewater rafters on the river near Lava Island having a blast and hopefully not swimming. Yet up-river a ways the Deschutes has time for calm, meandering sections suited to fly fishing, canoeing or a quick dip if you can handle the chilly waters. Frequented by families, the trail itself serves as a great day hike, especially on weekends and holidays, but be aware of other trail users regardless of the day. Bear in mind the total length from Meadow Camp Picnic Area to Sunriver and back is more than 20 miles. Since this ride is an "Out & Back" it is easily cut short using Ryan Ranch Meadow or Slough day use area as turn-around points. Pack a lunch because you'll find lots of scenic spots to take it all in. —*T.B*

Notes ... Access to cyclists on this trail is a sensitive issue. Individual actions represent mountain cyclists as a whole so please ride responsibly, in control, slow down and be sure to yield to all other trail users. Know the I.M.B.A. rules of the trail on p.63.

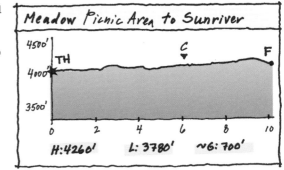

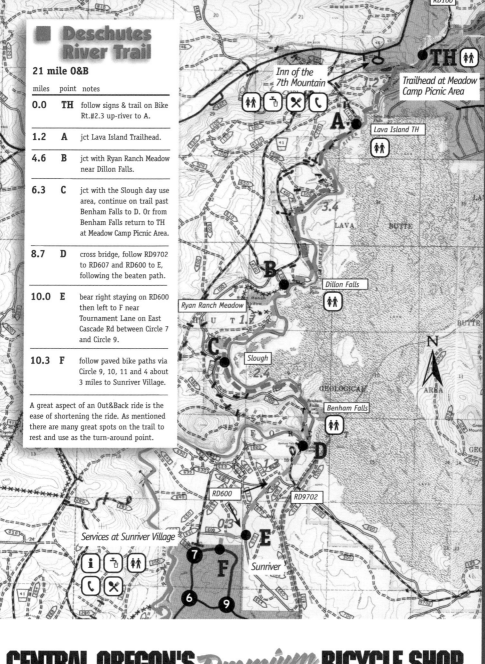

Deschutes River Trail

21 mile O&B

miles	point	notes
0.0	TH	follow signs & trail on Bike Rt.#2.3 up-river to A.
1.2	A	jct Lava Island Trailhead.
4.6	B	jct with Ryan Ranch Meadow near Dillon Falls.
6.3	C	jct with the Slough day use area, continue on trail past Benham Falls to D. Or from Benham Falls return to TH at Meadow Camp Picnic Area.
8.7	D	cross bridge, follow RD9702 to RD607 and RD600 to E, following the beaten path.
10.0	E	bear right staying on RD600 then left to F near Tournament Lane on East Cascade Rd between Circle 7 and Circle 9.
10.3	F	follow paved bike paths via Circle 9, 10, 11 and 4 about 3 miles to Sunriver Village.

A great aspect of an Out&Back ride is the ease of shortening the ride. As mentioned there are many great spots on the trail to rest and use as the turn-around point.

Inn of the 7th Mountain

Trailhead at Meadow Camp Picnic Area

Lava Island TH

Dillon Falls

Ryan Ranch Meadow

Slough

Benham Falls

RD600

RD9702

Services at Sunriver Village

Sunriver

Swede Ridge - Tumalo

14 Mile Loop

Tumalo Ridge, Swede Ridge, South Fork, Tumalo Falls Loop

- **TERRAIN** 95% singletrack, 5% dual track, seasonal sandy conditions, mild switchbacks, some incredible singletrack sections.

- **FITNESS** More difficult, mean elevation of 5600', vertical gain about 1200'.

- **LENGTH** 14 miles. More difficult to navigate. **SEASON** Summer – Late Fall. **USE** Moderate.

Getting There ... 10 miles. From town head through Bend's westside to 14th and Galveston. Continue straight on Galveston which shortly becomes Skyliners Road or RD4601. Follow Skyliners Road about 10 miles to junction with an informal winter Sno Park on the left and Tumalo Creek/Skyliners Trailhead. Look for trailhead signs in southwest end of parking area for Tumalo Creek Trail. Ride begins here.

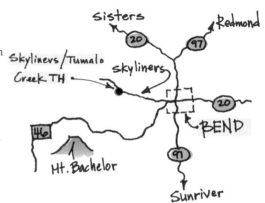

On the Trail ... The Tumalo Ridge, Swede Ridge, Swampy Lakes, South Fork, Tumalo Creek loop is definitely one of my all time favorite rides in Bend. Views of Tumalo Falls and the 1977 Bridge Creek forest fire from Tumalo Ridge are spectacular, plus incredible singletrack conditions give this trail all the qualities of a great ride. Choice singletrack with short technical sections and the solid climb from Tumalo Creek along Tumalo Ridge to Swede Ridge Shelter is an excellent workout. The Swede Ridge Shelter serves as a great spot to relax after the long climb from the Skyliners trailhead. Heavy tree canopy and the several creeks along the South Fork Trail keep the area lush and cool. Although the temptation to *"let 'em run"* from the Swampy Lakes Shelter down the Swampy Lakes/South Fork Trail is tempting, expect to see hikers, equestrians and other cyclists on the trail. If you see Don, Susan or the any of the Sunnyside Sports crew give 'em a special thanks for helping clear and maintain this trail.— *T.B*

Notes ... This trail has already seen complaints by other trail users for fast, reckless cycling. Slow it down, be courteous, keep it under control and yield to ALL other users.

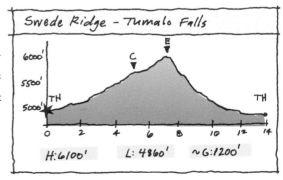

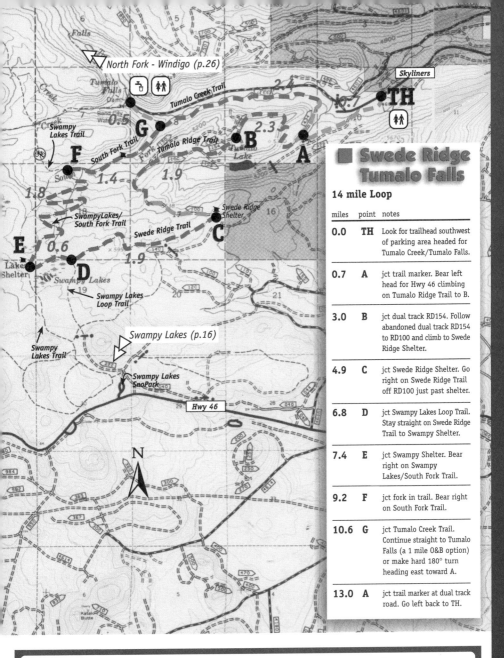

North Fork - Windigo (p.26)

Skyliners

Tumalo Creek Trail

Swampy Lakes Trail

South Fork Trail

Tumalo Ridge Trail

Swampy Lakes/South Fork Trail

Swede Ridge Shelter

Swede Ridge Trail

Swampy Lakes Loop Trail

Lake Shelter

Swampy Lakes (p.16)

Swampy Lakes Trail

Swampy Lakes SnoPark

Hwy 46

N

Swede Ridge Tumalo Falls

14 mile Loop

miles	point	notes
0.0	TH	Look for trailhead southwest of parking area headed for Tumalo Creek/Tumalo Falls.
0.7	A	jct trail marker. Bear left head for Hwy 46 climbing on Tumalo Ridge Trail to B.
3.0	B	jct dual track RD154. Follow abandoned dual track RD154 to RD100 and climb to Swede Ridge Shelter.
4.9	C	jct Swede Ridge Shelter. Go right on Swede Ridge Trail off RD100 just past shelter.
6.8	D	jct Swampy Lakes Loop Trail. Stay straight on Swede Ridge Trail to Swampy Shelter.
7.4	E	jct Swampy Shelter. Bear right on Swampy Lakes/South Fork Trail.
9.2	F	jct fork in trail. Bear right on South Fork Trail.
10.6	G	jct Tumalo Creek Trail. Continue straight to Tumalo Falls (a 1 mile O&B option) or make hard 180° turn heading east toward A.
13.0	A	jct trail marker at dual track road. Go left back to TH.

Cultus Lake Loop

12 Mile Loop

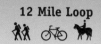

Winopee Lakes Trail, Many Lakes Trail and Deer Lake Trail

TERRAIN 75% dirt singletrack, 25% gravel and dirt dual track, smooth dirt singletrack, some minor technical sections – great as a short first-time intermediate ride.

FITNESS More difficult. Mean elevation 4700', total elevation gain about 400'.

LENGTH 12 miles. Easier to navigate. **SEASON** Summer – Fall. **USE** Light.

Getting There ... 46 miles. From town head through Bend's westside toward Mt. Bachelor on Cascade Lakes Highway RD46. Several miles past Mt. Bachelor, near the 44 mile mark from Bend, look for RD4635 on your right. Take RD4635 approximately 2 miles to Cultus Lake Campground. Park at the boat landing day use parking area. Ride begins here.

On the Trail ... We located the trailhead by riding our bikes to the north end of the

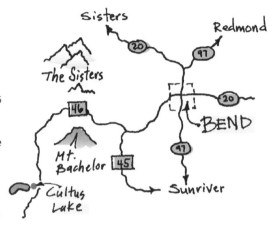

campground near the boat landing area. While staying close to the lake's edge, we joined the Winopee Lakes Trail which led us west around Cultus Lake. The trail begins on easier rolling terrain alongside the lake's northern shore and after several miles we found ourselves on the backside of Cultus Lake where a few boats were roped to the beach. We followed the trail to Deer Lake which offers a great spot to for some photos of deep blue waters stretching across to pines and spruce trees which touch the water's edge. After a few moments of relaxing, we jumped back on the saddle and rode down the smooth dirt Deer Lake Trail to Little Cultus Lake. Here the singletrack ended giving way to gravel and dirt roads. The pace of our ride picked up from Little Cultus Lake as we cruised along the roads back to Cultus Lake Campground completing the loop. During our research of this area we discovered the Lemish Lake loop closed due to a recent forest fire, the same fire you'll experience on the north shore of the Waldo Lake Trail. Steve Hayden, from the USDA Forest Service, suggested we mention this fun singletrack option, as it appears on the map, even though we did not include it in our narration. — *KR*

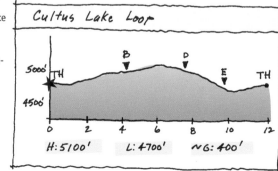

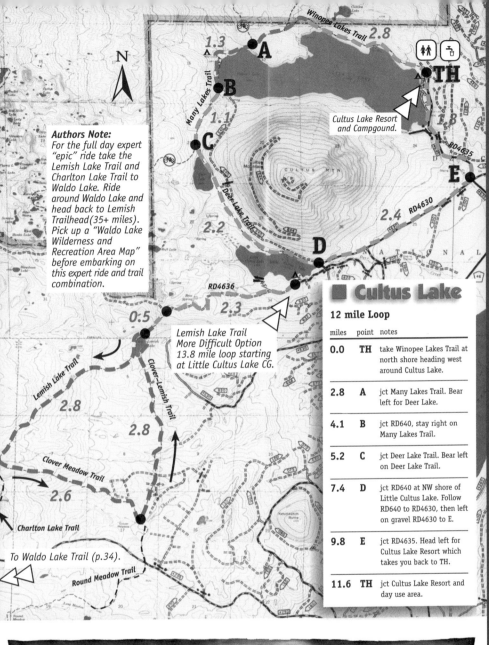

Authors Note:
For the full day expert "epic" ride take the Lemish Lake Trail and Charlton Lake Trail to Waldo Lake. Ride around Waldo Lake and head back to Lemish Trailhead(35+ miles). Pick up a "Waldo Lake Wilderness and Recreation Area Map" before embarking on this expert ride and trail combination.

Winopee Lakes Trail 2.8

1.3

A

Many Lakes Trail

B

1.1

C

1.8

RD4635

E

Deer Lake Trail

2.4 RD4630

2.2

D

Cultus Lake Resort and Campgound.

RD4636

2.3

0.5

Lemish Lake Trail
More Difficult Option
13.8 mile loop starting
at Little Cultus Lake CG.

Lemish Lake Trail

Clover-Lemish Trail

2.8

2.8

Clover Meadow Trail

2.6

Charlton Lake Trail

To Waldo Lake Trail (p.34).

Round Meadow Trail

■ Cultus Lake

12 mile Loop

miles	point	notes
0.0	TH	take Winopee Lakes Trail at north shore heading west around Cultus Lake.
2.8	A	jct Many Lakes Trail. Bear left for Deer Lake.
4.1	B	jct RD640, stay right on Many Lakes Trail.
5.2	C	jct Deer Lake Trail. Bear left on Deer Lake Trail.
7.4	D	jct RD640 at NW shore of Little Cultus Lake. Follow RD640 to RD4630, then left on gravel RD4630 to E.
9.8	E	jct RD4635. Head left for Cultus Lake Resort which takes you back to TH.
11.6	TH	jct Cultus Lake Resort and day use area.

North Fork - Flagline

The North Fork, Metolius-Windigo, Flagline, and South Fork Trail Loop

■ **TERRAIN** 100% singletrack, high alpine forest, technical climbs, challenging descents, both smooth and rocky surfaces — an incredible ride.

◆ **FITNESS** Most difficult. Continuous 7 mile climb, mean elevation 6000', total gain more than 2100'.

◆ **LENGTH** 20 miles. More difficult to navigate. **SEASON** Late Summer – Fall. **USE** Heavy*

*in areas

Getting There ... 13 miles. From downtown head for Bend's *westside*. At 14th and Galveston, go straight on Galveston which becomes Skyliners Road, RD4601. Follow Skyliners Road west about 10 miles to Tumalo Creek Road on right. Take Tumalo Creek Road, RD4603, about 2 miles to Tumalo Falls day use area. Look for signage for North Fork Trail and Tumalo Falls Overlook in the upper west portion of parking area. Ride begins here.

On the Trail ... No doubt this is one of the best rides in the area if you're up to the seven mile climb. Cyclists should give right-of-way to the horse and foot traffic also encountered in the area. The North Fork Trail is a gradual climb at the lower elevations and consists of a firm surface. A few miles into the ride we were faced with steeper grades and thinner air. Happy Valley is about 4 miles into the ride where the North Fork Trail junctions with the Metolius-Windigo Trail. Grinding up the steeper reaches of the last 3 miles of the climb past Happy Valley, along the Windigo Trail, took us south to the Flagline Trail with great views of Broken Top and Mt. Bachelor along the way. The descent on the Flagline Trail is one to ride every time you're in town. Loamy surface, heavy forest canopy, and a fun rhythm make it nearly perfect. The Swampy Shelter at the junction with the Swampy Lakes/South Fork Trail serves as a place to take a breather and have a snack. The descent from here continues at a steady pace, and after 8 miles, Tyler and I both felt this would be one of the best rides in the book. — *KR*

Notes ... We encountered snow on the trail in mid-July. Depending on the year, it may be present even later. Call the Fort Rock Ranger District (see p.63) and/or check www.SingletrackAnthology.com to confirm the upper trails are open and clear.

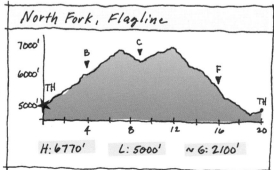

North Fork, Flagline

H: 6770'   L: 5000'   ~G: 2100'

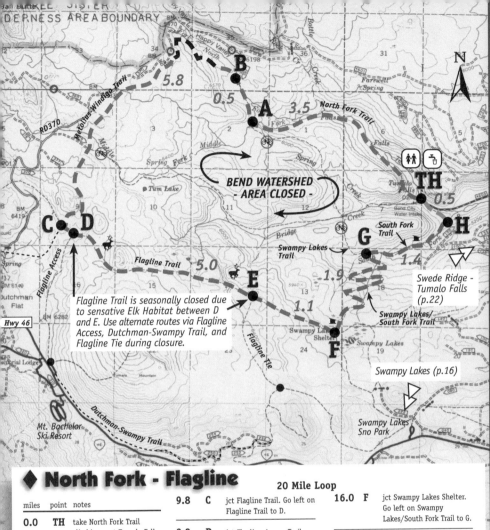

BEND WATERSHED - AREA CLOSED -

Flagline Trail is seasonally closed due to sensative Elk Habitat between D and E. Use alternate routes via Flagline Access, Dutchman-Swampy Trail, and Flagline Tie during closure.

Swede Ridge - Tumalo Falls (p.22)

Swampy Lakes (p.16)

◆ North Fork - Flagline

20 Mile Loop

miles	point	notes
0.0	TH	take North Fork Trail climbing past Tumalo Falls.
3.5	A	jct Swampy Lakes Trail into watershed, stay straight.
4.0	B	jct Happy Valley. Bear left, climbing steeply toward Todd Creek on M-W Trail to C.
9.8	C	jct Flagline Trail. Go left on Flagline Trail to D.
9.9	D	jct Flagline Access Trail. Continue straight on Flagline Trail to E.
14.9	E	jct Flagline Tie Trail. Continue straight to jct Swampy Lakes Trail then left on Swampy Lakes Trail to shelter.
16.0	F	jct Swampy Lakes Shelter. Go left on Swampy Lakes/South Fork Trail to G.
17.9	G	trail splits. Swampy Lakes Trail goes left into watershed. Bear right on South Fork Trail to H.
19.3	H	jct Tumalo Creek Trail. Bear left for Tumalo Falls and TH.

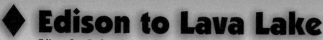

Edison to Lava Lake

Edison Sno Park to Lava Lake Campground

- **TERRAIN** 90% singletrack, 10% dual track, intense lava rock sections, steep climbs with rooted trail sections, long technical descents.

- **FITNESS** Most difficult, mean elevation 5300', total gain about 2500'.

- **LENGTH** 21 miles. More difficult to navigate. **SEASON** Summer – Late Fall. **USE** Light.

Getting There ... 21 miles. Take Cascades Lakes Hwy, RD46, westbound from Bend toward Mt. Bachelor. About 17 miles from town, turn left on RD45 heading for "LaPine, Sunriver, Edison SnoPark." Continue south on RD45 about 4 miles to Edison SnoPark on your right. Take the SnoPark access road another $1/4$ mile to parking lot. Look for the trailhead in the south end of the parking area. Ride begins here.

On the trail ... This trail challenges cyclists with intense rocky sections, a substantial amount of elevation change and some fast technical descents, all on a trail developed specifically for mountain biking. Paul Thomasberg wouldn't have it any other way on a trail he helped re-route and seasonally maintains. As with most high alpine trails the soils are fragile and become dusty pretty quickly. The trail starts out gradual then hits some technical rocky sections and climbs to the halfway point between the Edison SnoPark and Lava Lake Campground. Fast and steep singletrack lead down to Little Lava Lake, then mellows out substantially to the campground. Bring a couple of bucks for an ice cream sandwich from the convenience store at the campground. Fresh water and restrooms are available at Lava Lake campground as well. Don't relax too long as the trail back to Edison SnoPark is a 1,200' climb and just over 10 miles. One of the collapsible water bowls from Ruff Wear was ideal on this ride for my trail-savvy Australian Sheppard, Denali. — *T.B*

Notes ... If you are cycling with your dog be sure not to go too fast for too long on the descents. Also, there are grouchy, non-dog lovers out there, so be courteous and keep Fido out of trouble.

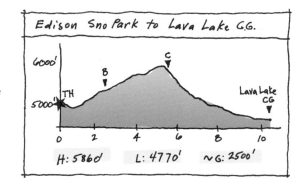

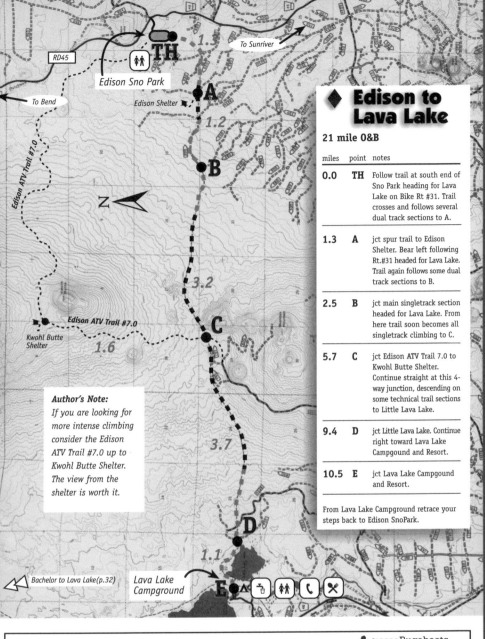

RD45

To Sunriver

Edison Sno Park

To Bend

Edison Shelter

TH

A
1.3

1.2

B

Z

Edison ATV Trail #7.0

3.2

C

Edison ATV Trail #7.0

Kwohl Butte
Shelter

1.6

Author's Note:

If you are looking for more intense climbing consider the Edison ATV Trail #7.0 up to Kwohl Butte Shelter. The view from the shelter is worth it.

3.7

D

1.1

Bachelor to Lava Lake(p.32)

Lava Lake
Campground

E

◆ Edison to Lava Lake

21 mile O&B

miles	point	notes
0.0	TH	Follow trail at south end of Sno Park heading for Lava Lake on Bike Rt #31. Trail crosses and follows several dual track sections to A.
1.3	A	jct spur trail to Edison Shelter. Bear left following Rt.#31 headed for Lava Lake. Trail again follows some dual track sections to B.
2.5	B	jct main singletrack section headed for Lava Lake. From here trail soon becomes all singletrack climbing to C.
5.7	C	jct Edison ATV Trail 7.0 to Kwohl Butte Shelter. Continue straight at this 4-way junction, descending on some technical trail sections to Little Lava Lake.
9.4	D	jct Little Lava Lake. Continue right toward Lava Lake Campgound and Resort.
10.5	E	jct Lava Lake Campgound and Resort.

From Lava Lake Campground retrace your steps back to Edison SnoPark.

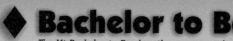 # Bachelor to Bend

The Mt. Bachelor to Bend ... the name says it all.

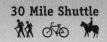

- **TERRAIN** 90% singletrack, 10% gravel and paved roads, technical trails sections, loamy dirt to dry, loose and rocky trail surfaces. Expect everything.
- **FITNESS** Most difficult, mean elevation about 5000', descending more than 3000'.
- **LENGTH** 30 miles. Most difficult to navigate. **SEASON** Summer – Fall **USE** Moderate.

Getting There ... 24 miles. Since this is a shuttle ride, before leaving Bend park one car at Shevlin Park (see p.14 for directions). Don't forget to bring the shuttle vehicle keys with you. Head out of town on Cascade Lakes Hwy, RD46, about 23 miles to RD370 on the right, approximately 2 or so miles past Mt. Bachelor. Follow signs for Todd Lake trailhead and day use area just up ahead. Ride begins here.

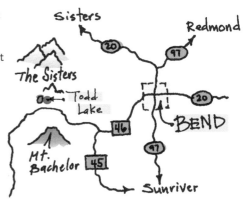

On the Trail ... This ride is one of the best and longest in the book with over 27 miles of mostly descending trail. This point-to-point ride is a combination of several rides offering the best of each. We jumped on our bikes at Todd Lake day use area just past Mt. Bachelor at approximately 6100'. Over the next few hours we meandered our way through incredible dense stands of Cascade mountain pine and fir trees, then descended to the eastern Oregon plateau depicted by drier soils, desert sage and manzanita. Snow, rivers, waterfalls, incredible views of the Three Sisters, Broken Top, Mt. Bachelor and ancient obsidian lava flows on the valley floor are a few highlights. By the time Tyler, Mike and I made it to our destination at Shevlin Park, 2500' below Todd Lake, we pondered how many climate zones we had descended through. The fun factor was definitely not a wonder. Did I mention this was one of the best rides in the book? One more thing ... did you remember the keys? Hope you have a hide-a-key as we did. — *KR*

Notes ... When planning a longer ride be certain to pack enough water, food and clothing for the trip. Be weather wise and plan for the worst, especially when riding in an alpine environment.

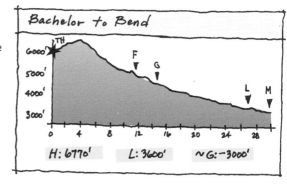

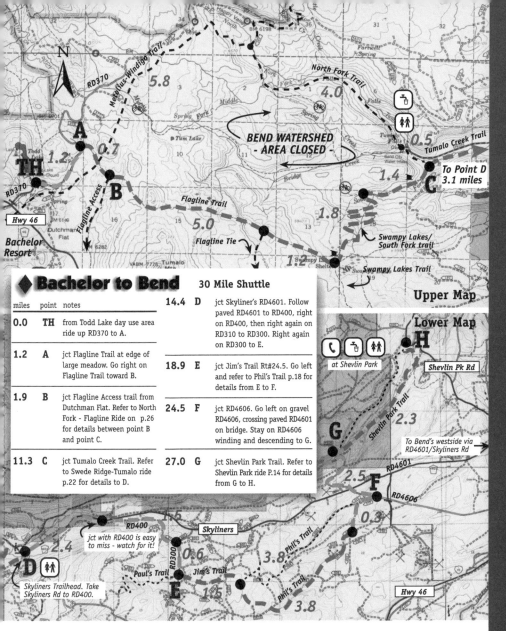

N

RD370

Metolius-Windigo Trail

5.8

North Fork Trail

4.0

RD370

A

0.7

1.2

TH

B

Flagline Access

Hwy 46

Bachelor Resort

Dutchman Flat

BEND WATERSHED - AREA CLOSED -

Tum Lake

Spring Fork

Bridge

Tumalo Creek Trail

0.5

To Point D
3.1 miles

1.4

C

Flagline Trail

5.0

1.8

Flagline Tie

1.2

Swampy Lakes/
South Fork trail

Swampy Lakes Trail

Upper Map

Lower Map

at Shevlin Park

H

Shevlin Pk Rd

Shevlin Park Trail

2.3

G

To Bend's westside via
RD4601/Skyliners Rd

2.5

F

RD4601

RD4606

0.3

◆ Bachelor to Bend — 30 Mile Shuttle

miles	point	notes
0.0	TH	from Todd Lake day use area ride up RD370 to A.
1.2	A	jct Flagline Trail at edge of large meadow. Go right on Flagline Trail toward B.
1.9	B	jct Flagline Access trail from Dutchman Flat. Refer to North Fork - Flagline Ride on p.26 for details between point B and point C.
11.3	C	jct Tumalo Creek Trail. Refer to Swede Ridge-Tumalo ride p.22 for details to D.
14.4	D	jct Skyliner's RD4601. Follow paved RD4601 to RD400, right on RD400, then right again on RD310 to RD300. Right again on RD300 to E.
18.9	E	jct Jim's Trail Rt#24.5. Go left and refer to Phil's Trail p.18 for details from E to F.
24.5	F	jct RD4606. Go left on gravel RD4606, crossing paved RD4601 on bridge. Stay on RD4606 winding and descending to G.
27.0	G	jct Shevlin Park Trail. Refer to Shevlin Park ride P.14 for details from G to H.

RD400

jct with RD400 is easy to miss - watch for it!

2.4

D

Skyliners Trailhead. Take
Skyliners Rd to RD400.

RD300

Skyliners

0.6

Paul's Trail

Jim's Trail

E

1.5

3.8

Phil's Trail

3.8

Phil's Trail

Hwy 46

Bachelor to Lava Lake

Sparks Lake Area to Lava Lake Campground - Options

■ **TRAIL** 13 miles of high alpine singletrack, dual track and paved options. Rocky sections, sand, heavy horse traffic contributes to seasonally rough trail conditions.

◆ **FITNESS** Most difficult O&B or Longest Loop. Mean elevation 5100', total descent about 1200'. More difficult medium or shorter loops.

◆ **LENGTH** 12 miles one-way to Lava Lake. **SEASON** Summer – Fall. **USE** Moderate. Loop option total: 8 to 25 miles. O&B option: 25 miles.

Getting There ... 23-25 miles. From Bend take Cascade Lakes Hwy, RD46, about 22 miles to RD390 on your left, about a mile past Mt. Bachelor Ski Area. Find a suitable place to park off of RD390. Ride begins here.

Trailhead Option: Continue down RD46 another 2 miles to Soda Creek campground and day use area. Park here then ride back up RD46 to RD390, eliminating this climb at the end of the ride.

On the Trail ... This ride requires a certain degree of technical ability, forethought and navigation skills as many options exist. We chose to park at Soda Creek day use area then ride back up RD46 to RD390 in order to pick up the Metolius-Windigo Trail. Once on singletrack, the trail starts with a rocky surface mixed with sandy conditions typical of alpine trails. Rolling for a short bit then quickly descending, we hit some tight corners testing our skills as the trail meandered around old blow-down snags and through a sparse overhead forest canopy. Further down the trail toward Lava Lake, the ride flattened out for a bit but continually put our suspension under a load due to the trail's popularity with horseback riders. Keep horse traffic in mind when riding due to potential encounters and adverse trail conditions. We kept steering south toward Lava Lake at all junction points while descending most of the 12 miles. A swim, a soda and fresh drinking water awaits at the Lava Lake Resort convenience store. However, don't relax too long because either way you ride, you have a minimum of 11 miles back to your vehicle. — *KR*

Notes ... Yes, its true, mountain weather changes rapidly. We went from sunny warm conditions to pachinko ball hail stones in less than 20 minutes. And there's not much overhead protection along Hwy 46.

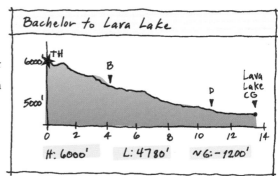

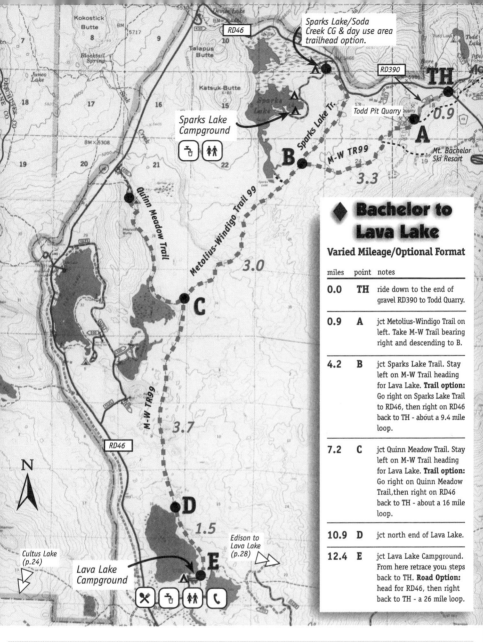

Sparks Lake/Soda Creek CG & day use area trailhead option.

RD46

RD390

TH

Todd Pit Quarry

0.9

A

Sparks Lake Tr.

M-W TR99

3.3

Mt. Bachelor Ski Resort

Sparks Lake Campground

B

Quinn Meadow Trail

Metolius-Windigo Trail 99

3.0

C

M-W TR99

3.7

RD46

D

1.5

E

Edison to Lava Lake (p.28)

Cultus Lake (p.24)

Lava Lake Campground

N

◆ Bachelor to Lava Lake

Varied Mileage/Optional Format

miles	point	notes
0.0	TH	ride down to the end of gravel RD390 to Todd Quarry.
0.9	A	jct Metolius-Windigo Trail on left. Take M-W Trail bearing right and descending to B.
4.2	B	jct Sparks Lake Trail. Stay left on M-W Trail heading for Lava Lake. **Trail option:** Go right on Sparks Lake Trail to RD46, then right on RD46 back to TH - about a 9.4 mile loop.
7.2	C	jct Quinn Meadow Trail. Stay left on M-W Trail heading for Lava Lake. **Trail option:** Go right on Quinn Meadow Trail, then right on RD46 back to TH - about a 16 mile loop.
10.9	D	jct north end of Lava Lake.
12.4	E	jct Lava Lake Campground. From here retrace your steps back to TH. **Road Option:** head for RD46, then right back to TH - a 26 mile loop.

 # Waldo Lake
The Incredibly Scenic Waldo Lake Trail

 20 Mile Loop

- ■ **TERRAIN** 100% singletrack, high alpine forest, mostly dirt trail with short technical descents, some rocky areas, stream crossings. Expect anything.
- ◆ **FITNESS** Most difficult, mean elevation 5300', total gain about 400'.
- ◆ **LENGTH** 20 miles. Easier to navigate.   **SEASON** Summer – Fall.   **USE** Heavy.

Getting There ... 70 miles. Take Cascade Lakes Hwy, RD46, about 60 miles to RD4290. Go right on gravel RD4290, which is an extremely rough gravel road for about 8 miles to RD5898. Go right on RD5898 for 2 miles then make a right on RD515 heading for N. Waldo Lake Campground. Head for the boat launch parking area. Look for trailhead in north end of parking area. Ride begins here. Consult your local map for smoother routes from Sunriver and Eugene to Waldo Lake, avoiding RD4290.

On the Trail ... The Waldo Lake ride is a classic scenic loop around one of the most beautiful and unique lakes in Oregon, making the longer drive from Bend well worth it. Waldo Lake, fed solely by snow melt waters and coupled with its high altitude location, near 5500', result in one of the purest, clearest lakes in the world. Since the lake is almost always in view from the trail, depths of up to 100' are visible from places high on the trail. The trail itself is easy to navigate and has everything from beginner to expert terrain. We forded streams, climbed rocky outcrops and even plowed through snowy sections in early August. The 1996 burn area on the north end of the lake is an incredible contrast of black tree snags and soot with intense green vegetation flourishing in the fertile soils. When finished, Kent and I agreed we had chosen the best mode of transportation to take it all in. Camping is available at several locations around the lake and at the trailhead, so bring some camping equipment or take along the panniers to make a weekend out of it. Reservations may be needed for camping during peak season. — *T.B.*

Notes ... Plan ahead when driving longer distances for rides. Weather, trail, automobile and bike conditions are well worth looking at before heading for the trailhead.

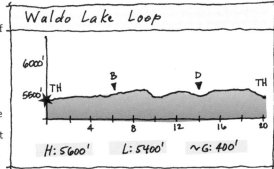

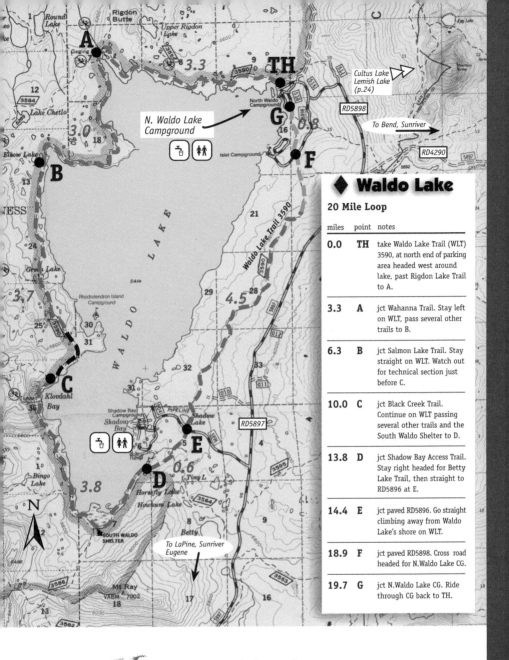

N. Waldo Lake Campground

♦ **Waldo Lake**

20 Mile Loop

miles	point	notes
0.0	TH	take Waldo Lake Trail (WLT) 3590, at north end of parking area headed west around lake, past Rigdon Lake Trail to A.
3.3	A	jct Wahanna Trail. Stay left on WLT, pass several other trails to B.
6.3	B	jct Salmon Lake Trail. Stay straight on WLT. Watch out for technical section just before C.
10.0	C	jct Black Creek Trail. Continue on WLT passing several other trails and the South Waldo Shelter to D.
13.8	D	jct Shadow Bay Access Trail. Stay right headed for Betty Lake Trail, then straight to RD5896 at E.
14.4	E	jct paved RD5896. Go straight climbing away from Waldo Lake's shore on WLT.
18.9	F	jct paved RD5898. Cross road headed for N.Waldo Lake CG.
19.7	G	jct N.Waldo Lake CG. Ride through CG back to TH.

Sisters
Oregon

top — Brad's Trail near Squaw Creek (p.46). **photo** Bob Woodward
above — Blue waters of Clear Lake on McKenzie River Trail (p.48). **photo** Bob Woodward
opposite — Looking north towards Mt.Jefferson near Cache Mountain (p.44). **photo** Bob Woodward

Suttle Lake

🚶🚶 🚴 **13 Mile O&B/Loop**

The Suttle Lake Tie and Suttle Lake Loop Trails

- **TERRAIN** easier trail with 70% singletrack, 25% abandoned dual tracks, some technical-sections, seasonal sandy and dusty conditions.
- **FITNESS** easier, mean elevation 3400', total gain about 350'.
- **LENGTH** 13 miles. Easier to navigate.   **SEASON** Spring – Late Fall.   **USE** Heavy.

Getting There ... 10 miles. Head west out of downtown Sisters on Hwy20 for Santiam Pass. Continue past Black Butte Ranch to intersection with RD14 and RD2060. Turn left on RD2060 and look for the Suttle Tie trailhead in a small parking area on your immediate right. "Roads to Trails" signage should be present with other signage indicating the Suttle Lake Tie trail. Ride begins here.

On the Trail ... The Suttle Lake Tie trail is a "Roads to Trails" project taking abandoned forest roads and creating established hiking and biking trails. The Suttle Tie trail is clearly marked with 4x4 "Roads to Trails" posts and is a series of dual track and singletrack sections leading to the popular Suttle Lake recreation area. Gentle dual track cruising with some occasional singletrack dips and curves make for a solid beginner ride, although the scenery and buffed out singletrack around the lake will appeal to even veteran cyclists. Water, restrooms and great car-camping spots are abundant at Suttle Lake, but if you are planning an overnight stay you may want to call ahead to reserve a camp site. The loop around Suttle Lake is very popular and the trail is clearly marked. We managed to get a bit off course once we completed the loop around the lake while trying to find the Suttle Tie Trail again. However, we found it just south of the Suttle Lake Resort lodge and across Lake Creek. Suttle Lake is a great spot to camp and also ride the Cache Mountain Trail (p.44) as well. — *T.B.*

Notes ... Due to the popularity of Suttle Lake beware of other users especially campers. We here in the late fall and saw no one else during the ride.

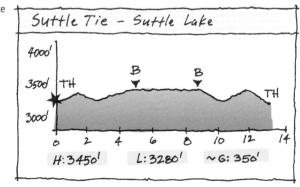

Suttle Tie - Suttle Lake

H: 3450'   L: 3280'   ~G: 350'

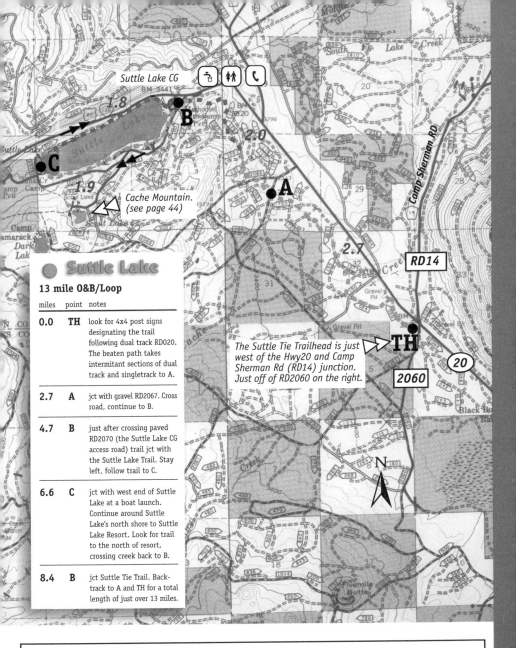

Suttle Lake CG

Cache Mountain.
(see page 44)

The Suttle Tie Trailhead is just
west of the Hwy20 and Camp
Sherman Rd (RD14) junction.
Just off of RD2060 on the right.

RD14

2060

20

N

Suttle Lake

13 mile O&B/Loop

miles	point	notes
0.0	TH	look for 4x4 post signs designating the trail following dual track RD020. The beaten path takes intermitant sections of dual track and singletrack to A.
2.7	A	jct with gravel RD2067. Cross road, continue to B.
4.7	B	just after crossing paved RD2070 (the Suttle Lake CG access road) trail jct with the Suttle Lake Trail. Stay left, follow trail to C.
6.6	C	jct with west end of Suttle Lake at a boat launch. Continue around Suttle Lake's north shore to Suttle Lake Resort. Look for trail to the north of resort, crossing creek back to B.
8.4	B	jct Suttle Tie Trail. Back-track to A and TH for a total length of just over 13 miles.

Peterson Ridge

🚶🚶 🚴 **15 Mile O&B/Loop***

Peterson Ridge Intermediate Loop with Beginner Loop Option

- **TERRAIN** 85% singletrack, 15% dual track, seasonal dusty and sandy conditions. Technical rocky climbs and descents on more difficult loop option.

- **FITNESS** Rt#2 more difficult loop, mean elevation 3500', climbs about 500'. Rt#1 easier loop.

- **LENGTH** 15 miles. More difficult to navigate. **SEASON** Spring – Late Fall. **USE** Heavy. *Option: 6 mile easier loop.

Getting There ...1 mile. It's actually less than a mile to the singletrack! Park in Sisters and ride south less than a mile on East Elm Street to the junction of Tyee Drive and RD16, just across the Squaw Creek bridge. The Peterson Ridge trailhead is on the south-east corner of Tyee Drive and RD16. It's that easy.

On the Trail ... The Peterson Ridge trail starts out winding along a surface of sand and river rock making for some tricky trail conditions during dry spells, however, after a fresh rain the trail is exceptional. Rolling terrain sums up the first few miles on the easier loop option. At approximately 2½ miles we came to Squaw Creek irrigation canal where the more difficult upper loop option begins. Staying right on the north side of the canal took us back down the slope and joined the easier loop option we had ridden already (see the map). Crossing the canal, the trail continues to climb up into the pines on the more difficult loop option. I call this type of loop a classic lollipop loop ... refer to the map ... do you see it? Anyway, we climbed up to the area known as Peterson Ridge with some incredible views of the North, Middle and South Sisters. After taking in the views and a few photos, we descended on the trail we had climbed earlier, back down to the irrigation canal completing the upper lollipop loop. Sisters is just under 2 miles from here back to the trailhead. —*KR*

Notes ... Seat height and angle are very important for an efficient ride. Check for about a 90% extended leg on each pedal stroke while seated.

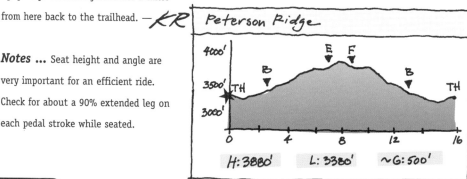

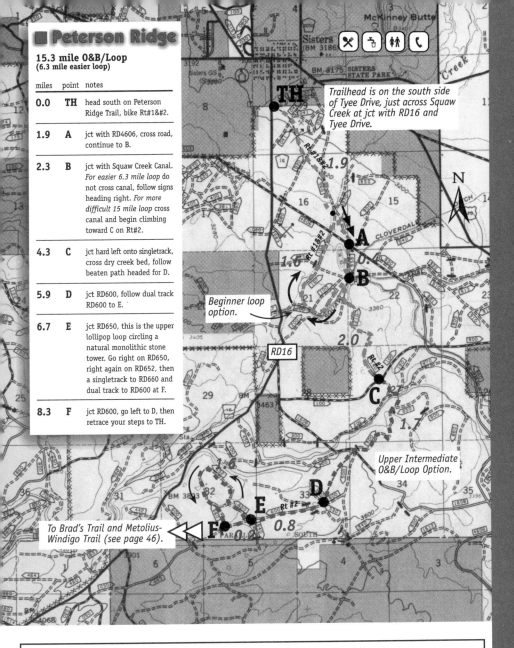

■ Peterson Ridge

15.3 mile O&B/Loop
(6.3 mile easier loop)

miles	point	notes
0.0	TH	head south on Peterson Ridge Trail, bike Rt#1&#2.
1.9	A	jct with RD4606, cross road, continue to B.
2.3	B	jct with Squaw Creek Canal. *For easier 6.3 mile loop do not cross canal, follow signs heading right. For more difficult 15 mile loop cross canal and begin climbing toward C on Rt#2.*
4.3	C	jct hard left onto singletrack, cross dry creek bed, follow beaten path headed for D.
5.9	D	jct RD600, follow dual track RD600 to E.
6.7	E	jct RD650, this is the upper lollipop loop circling a natural monolithic stone tower. Go right on RD650, right again on RD652, then a singletrack to RD660 and dual track to RD600 at F.
8.3	F	jct RD600, go left to D, then retrace your steps to TH.

Trailhead is on the south side of Tyee Drive, just across Squaw Creek at jct with RD16 and Tyee Drive.

Beginner loop option.

Upper Intermediate O&B/Loop Option.

To Brad's Trail and Metolius-Windigo Trail (see page 46).

Upper Three Creeks

10.5 Mile Loop

Upper Three Creeks and Metolius–Windigo Trail

- **TERRAIN** 50% dirt singletrack, 45% dual track, 5% paved road, alpine forest riding with seasonal sandy and dusty conditions, technical rocky sections, exposed roots, fun descents.
- **FITNESS** More difficult. Mean elevation 5500', total gain about 1100' in 5 miles.
- **LENGTH** 10.5 miles. Easier to navigate.   **SEASON** Spring – Late Fall.   **USE** Moderate.

Getting There ... 11 miles. Take East Elm Street heading south out of Sisters. Just after crossing Squaw Creek, East Elm Street becomes RD16. Follow RD16 eleven miles to dirt RD700 on your right, located just past paved RD1610 at the entrance to the Upper Three Creeks SnoPark. At the time RD700 was gated. We parked on the right just outside the gate. Ride starts here. Look for winter recreation signs directing you toward Three Creeks Lake Trail on RD700.

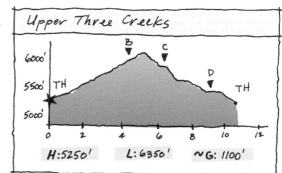

On the Trail ... The Upper Three Creeks trail skirts the edge of the Three Sisters Wilderness boundary, so the ride is extremely beautiful. There are repeated views of the Three Sisters mountains and the high plains to the east. The scenery during the 5 mile climb makes it less monotonous, but not easy due to the 5500' mean elevation. We finished the climb on a short section of pavement, on RD16, anticipating the euphoric descent promised by our local trail master and good guy Brad Boyd of EuroSports. I remember letting go an occasional "whoopee" during the 5 mile descent. With meadows and mountains all around us, the scene was unbelievable. An amazing trail, fast and technical with rocky sections and tree roots. Below the rocky upper reaches, the trail dramatically changes to smooth dirt singletrack allowing a more relaxed riding, despite some quick turns. In general, the trail is well marked, however be attentive at junctions to stay on designated bike trails. *KR*

Notes ... Due to the Wilderness area west of Squaw Creek other trail users may express concern for your presence. Smile, be courteous and show them our map if necessary. The bike route skirts the Wilderness area making it 100% legal.

Upper Three Creeks

10.5 mile loop

miles	point	notes
0.0	TH	follow RD700 climbing 4 miles, crossing numerous other dual track roads to A.
4.0	A	jct paved RD16, go right to Park Meadow/Metolius-Windigo Trailhead, a short bit past where RD16 turn to gravel.
4.5	B	jct Park Meadow Trailhead on the right, follow Park Meadow Trail/Metolius-Windigo Trail to C.
6.7	C	jct fork in trail. Bear right staying on Metolius-Windigo Trail. Park Meadow Trail goes straight, crossing Squaw Creek into Three Sisters Wilderness Area which is closed to bikes.
9.0	D	jct RD740, go right on dual track road to RD700 at E.
9.3	E	jct RD700, go left and descend back to TH.

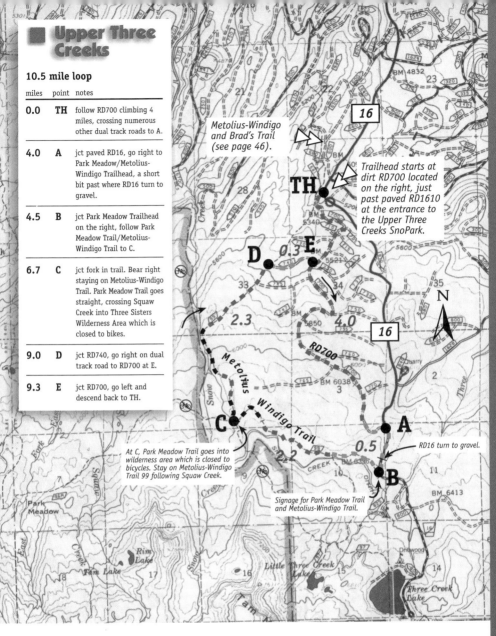

Metolius-Windigo and Brad's Trail (see page 46).

Trailhead starts at dirt RD700 located on the right, just past paved RD1610 at the entrance to the Upper Three Creeks SnoPark.

At C, Park Meadow Trail goes into wilderness area which is closed to bicycles. Stay on Metolius-Windigo Trail 99 following Squaw Creek.

Signage for Park Meadow Trail and Metolius-Windigo Trail.

RD16 turn to gravel.

◆ Cache Mountain

🚶🚶 🚲 🏇 **13 Mile L**

Scout Lake, Dark Lake, Cache Mountain Loop

◆ **TERRAIN** 50% dirt singletrack on descent, 50% gravel and dirt dual track on climb. Some steep descents near the summit, switchbacks ... great descent!

◆ **FITNESS** Most difficult. Mean elevation 5600', total gain about 2000'.

■ **LENGTH** 13 miles. Most difficult to navigate. **SEASON** Summer – Late Fall. **USE** Moderate.

Getting There ... 15 miles. From Sisters head west on Hwy 20 for Santiam Pass. At about 13.5 miles turn left at Suttle Lake Campground. Follow road just over 1 mile then turn left on RD2066 heading for Scout Lake. Follow RD2066 about a half mile to RD700 and turn right heading again toward Scout Lake. Continue another ¼ mile to Scout Lake. Look for trail at lake's south shore. Ride begins here.

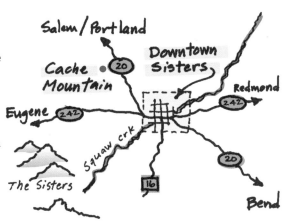

On the Trail ... The ride starts on singletrack, skirts Scout Lake at the beginning, which seems pretty tame, but then rapidly climbs for the first mile. The best advise here is to be warmed up before you start this ride, as we were not. The crisp morning air penetrated deep into our lungs making it really tough. At about 1.5 miles we came to a forest road where the climb seemed less steep but still headed upward, providing not even a glimmer of a break during the entire eight miles to the top. About seven miles of grinding was almost enough and I remember needing a change of grade ... down! At a bit over eight miles we found just that. For the remainder of this ride good brakes and nerves of steel were in order on some of the trail. Pedaling during the descent to Dark Lake was optional and hardly needed for nearly four miles! The initial eight miles were tough but the descent made it worth the effort – especially the incredible views from the top. — *KR*

Notes ... Even though the singletrack descent starts before the top of Cache Mountain we recommend going the extra distance to the top for the panoramic views of Mt. Bachelor, Broken Top, The Sisters, Mt. Washington, Mt. Jefferson and Mt. Hood, all visible on a clear day.

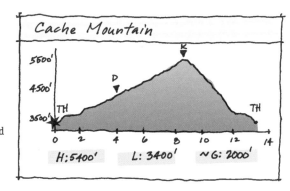

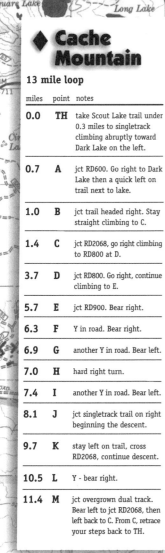

◆ Cache Mountain

13 mile loop

miles	point	notes
0.0	TH	take Scout Lake trail under 0.3 miles to singletrack climbing abruptly toward Dark Lake on the left.
0.7	A	jct RD600. Go right to Dark Lake then a quick left on trail next to lake.
1.0	B	jct trail headed right. Stay straight climbing to C.
1.4	C	jct RD2068, go right climbing to RD800 at D.
3.7	D	jct RD800. Go right, continue climbing to E.
5.7	E	jct RD900. Bear right.
6.3	F	Y in road. Bear right.
6.9	G	another Y in road. Bear left.
7.0	H	hard right turn.
7.4	I	another Y in road. Bear left.
8.1	J	jct singletrack trail on right beginning the descent.
9.7	K	stay left on trail, cross RD2068, continue descent.
10.5	L	Y - bear right.
11.4	M	jct overgrown dual track. Bear left to jct RD2068, then left back to C. From C, retrace your steps back to TH.

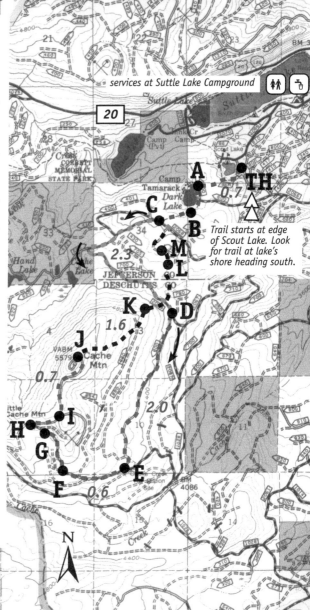

services at Suttle Lake Campground

Trail starts at edge of Scout Lake. Look for trail at lake's shore heading south.

Windigo-Brad's Trail

26 Mile Shuttle

Metolius–Windigo Trail, Brad's Trail to Peterson Ridge Trail to Sisters

◆ **TERRAIN** 80% dirt singletrack, 20% abandoned dual track. Alpine forest riding with seasonal sand and dusty conditions, technical rocky sections, exposed roots, fun descents.

■ **FITNESS** More difficult. Mean elevation 4000', total descent about 2000'.

◆ **LENGTH** 26 miles. Most difficult to navigate. **SEASON** Late Spring – Late Fall. **USE** Light.

Getting There ... 14 miles. Leave a shuttle vehicle in Sisters then take East Elm Street heading south out of town. East Elm becomes RD16; continue 14 miles to the Upper Three Creeks SnoPark shortly past where RD16 turns into gravel. Park in west end of the SnoPark area. Ride begins here. Look for winter recreation and trailhead signs directing you toward Park Meadow and the Metolius-Windigo Trail 99.

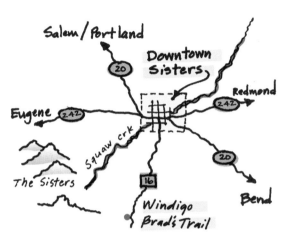

On the Trail ... After riding portions of the Metolius-Windigo Trail we were ready to take it all the way to Sisters. Legend has it Squaw creek is usually running too big to safely ford about half way to Sisters on the Windigo Trail. We discovered Brad's Trail allows us to join the Metolius-Windigo Trail, without crossing Squaw Creek, with the Peterson Ridge Trail making an incredible combination. Like the "Bachelor to Bend" ride (p.30), Kent and I counted several different micro-climatic zones while on the trail. Riding conditions varied from the rocky, loose, teeth clinching trail near the top of the Upper Three Creeks area to the loamy and buffed out "yeehaw" singletrack on the lower reaches of the Metolius-Windigo Trail and Brad's Trail. Hugging Squaw Creek's eastern shore, Brad's Trail provides a link between the Metolius-Windigo Trail and the Peterson Ridge Trail (p.40). Beautiful scenery, great singletrack, a good bit of distance traveled and a mostly descending ride make this combination of trails a true adventure. —*T.B*

Notes ... Since this is a "shuttle" ride don't forget the keys to your shuttle vehicle. Otherwise you might have to convince Brad to give you a ride back to your car. Due to other access points to RD16, shorter loops are possible from this ride.

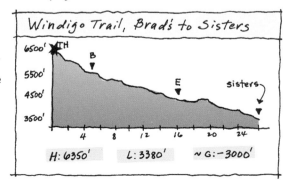

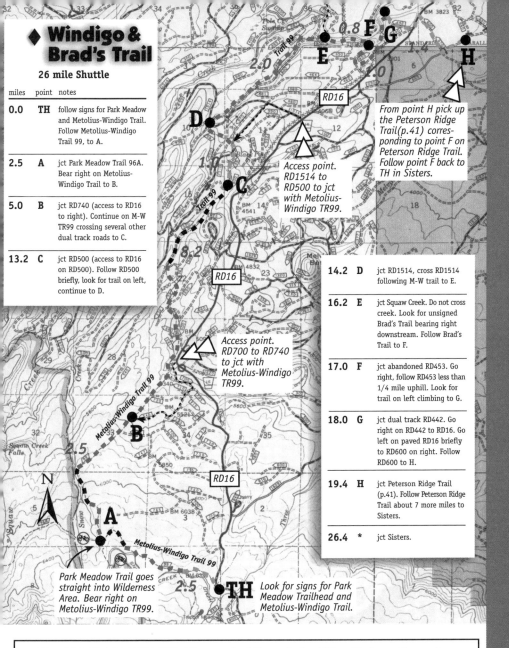

◆ Windigo & Brad's Trail

26 mile Shuttle

miles	point	notes
0.0	TH	follow signs for Park Meadow and Metolius-Windigo Trail. Follow Metolius-Windigo Trail 99, to A.
2.5	A	jct Park Meadow Trail 96A. Bear right on Metolius-Windigo Trail to B.
5.0	B	jct RD740 (access to RD16 to right). Continue on M-W TR99 crossing several other dual track roads to C.
13.2	C	jct RD500 (access to RD16 on RD500). Follow RD500 briefly, look for trail on left, continue to D.
14.2	D	jct RD1514, cross RD1514 following M-W trail to E.
16.2	E	jct Squaw Creek. Do not cross creek. Look for unsigned Brad's Trail bearing right downstream. Follow Brad's Trail to F.
17.0	F	jct abandoned RD453. Go right, follow RD453 less than 1/4 mile uphill. Look for trail on left climbing to G.
18.0	G	jct dual track RD442. Go right on RD442 to RD16. Go left on paved RD16 briefly to RD600 on right. Follow RD600 to H.
19.4	H	jct Peterson Ridge Trail (p.41). Follow Peterson Ridge Trail about 7 more miles to Sisters.
26.4	*	jct Sisters.

Access point. RD1514 to RD500 to jct with Metolius-Windigo TR99.

From point H pick up the Peterson Ridge Trail(p.41) corresponding to point F on Peterson Ridge Trail. Follow point F back to TH in Sisters.

Access point. RD700 to RD740 to jct with Metolius-Windigo TR99.

Park Meadow Trail goes straight into Wilderness Area. Bear right on Metolius-Windigo TR99.

Look for signs for Park Meadow Trailhead and Metolius-Windigo Trail.

McKenzie River Trail

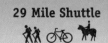

The McKenzie National Wild and Scenic River Recreation Trail

◆ **TERRAIN** 95% singletrack. Everything from paved singletrack through lava fields to incredible buffed out singletrack, waterfalls, old growth trees, clear lakes ... you name it!

◆ **FITNESS** Most difficult due to length. Mean elevation 2400', total descent about 1600'.

◆ **LENGTH** 29 miles. More difficult to navigate. **SEASON** Summer – Fall. **USE** Heavy in areas.

Getting There ... 31-53 miles.

From Sisters take Hwy20 about 29 miles to Santiam Pass and junction with Hwy126. Take Hwy126 heading for "McKenzie River Recreation Area/Eugene". The ideal place to leave a shuttle vehicle is in the town of McKenzie Bridge, near the convenience store, about 24 miles from Santiam Pass. The upper trailhead begins next to Fish Lake Creek on RD2676 about 22 miles back up Hwy126 from McKenzie Bridge. Look Old Santiam Wagon Road signs on the south side of Hwy126 at upper TH.

On the Trail ...

The McKenzie River Trail is definitely one of the the top five mountain biking trails in Oregon, so the drive, regardless of where you are coming, is well worth it. Old growth groves of douglas fir as well as mountain hemlock, red cedar, and madrones are plentiful. Geologically recent lava flows are common near the top of the McKenzie River trail, making for interesting topography including lava tubes left behind from fallen trees in the lava. These lava flows also forced the McKenzie River to be completely absorbed in the porous lava rock near Trail Bridge Reservoir, only to resurface at Tamolitch Falls. Incredible waterfalls and rapids make for numerous picturesque stops along the way. Aside from the captivating surroundings the trail itself will test your abilities through a variety of conditions. While buffed out singletrack of loamy mountain soils keep you smiling, short, steep descents, lava rock, narrow bridges (most too narrow to ride), and sharp corners will test your mettle. Bring your camera and extra film. If you don't you'll wish you had. – *T.B*

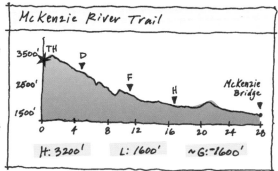

◆ McKenzie River

29.0 mile Shuttle

miles	point	notes
0.0	TH	Look for trail to the south of Hwy126 on RD2676. Take trail heading south to A.
1.0	A	jct Clear Lake Trail. Go left at bridge on McKenzie River Trail (MRT) headed for B. Paved and technical trail through lava roack ahead.
3.5	B	jct Clear Lake Trail again, follow signs for Sahallie Falls thru Cold Water Cove CG.
4.0	C	jct Hwy126. Cross highway, follow MRT and signs for Carmen Resevoir. Use caution due to cliffs in area!
5.4	D	jct Waterfalls Trail S. jct, bear right for Tamolitch Falls.
9.0	E	jct Tamolitch Falls (Blue Pool), follow MRT.
11.0	F	jct RD655, continue crossing several gravel roads.
12.2	G	jct Trail Bridge CG, look for MRT on left, head for Trail Bridge Resevoir.
16.3	H	jct Dear Creek, cross another road then cross Frissell Creek headed for I.
19.8	I	jct gravel RD2650, go left on RD2650, cross river, pick up trail on right.
24.1	J	jct Paradise CG, follow MRT.
27.0	K	jct Hwy126, end of trail. Bear right on Hwy126 about 2 more miles to the town of McKenzie Bridge.

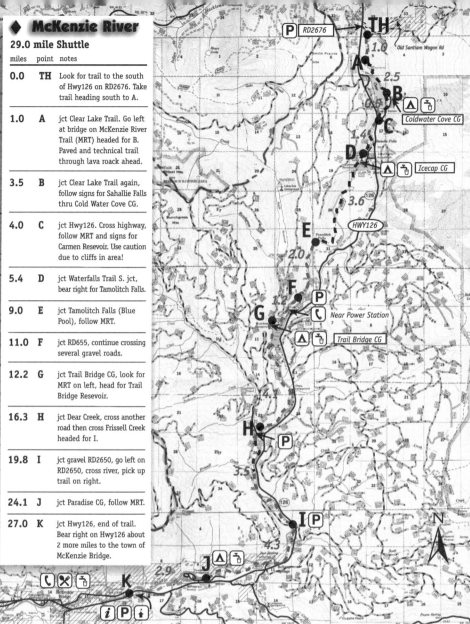

Sunriver

Oregon

above —Looking south from Newberry Crater Rim Trail (p.60). **photo** Bob Woodward
opposite — Fall colors along the Deschutes River Trail near Ryan Ranch Meadow (p.58). **photo** Bob Woodward

Benham Falls

Sunriver Village to Benham Falls

🚶🚶 🚴 **11 Mile O&B**

- **TERRAIN** 60% paved bike paths within Sunriver, 30% dual track roads, 10% singletrack.

- **FITNESS** Easier, mean elevation 4200', total gain about 250'.

- **LENGTH** 11 miles. Easier to navigate. **SEASON** Year Round*. **USE** Extreme.
  *winter weather permitting

Getting There ... The Sunriver community is located about 15 miles south of downtown Bend on Hwy97 and just 18 miles east of Mt. Bachelor. Heading south from Bend, take a right on S. Century Drive, RD40, toward Sunriver off Hwy97. Follow S. Century Drive about 2.5 miles to Abbot Drive, then turn right again. Follow signs for Sunriver Village where trail narration begins. Please note vehicle parking is restricted to public areas only within Sunriver.

On the Trail ... From the Sunriver Village Mall take the paved bike paths to East Cascade Road between Circle 7 and 9 to the northern Sunriver boundary. We found the best route was to take the bike paths paralleling Beaver Drive to Circle 11. It may be wise to pick up a free Sunriver area map to help navigate within Sunriver. Follow the bike paths paralleling East Cascade Road via Circle 10 and 9 taking you to north past Tournament Lane to a sign "Path to Benham Falls." This is a great ride for first time mountain bikers who want go off-road. Plus the destination, Benham Falls along the Deschutes River, is Mother Nature's beauty and power at her best. The contrast between Sunriver's smooth paved bike paths compared to the singletrack and dual track roads of the Deschutes National Forest surrounding Sunriver is quite abrupt. Pine trees, obsidian lava flows, and the rushing Deschutes river waters are some highlights on the ride. If you are feeling adventurous continue a bit past Benham Falls on the more challenging singletrack of the Deschutes River Trail (p.58). — T.B

Notes ... Remember to ride in control at all times. Bicyclists must slow down and yield to all other trail users.

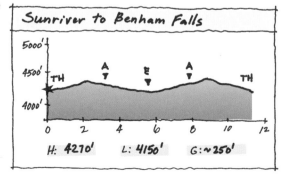

Sunriver to Benham Falls

H: 4270'   L: 4150'   G: ~250'

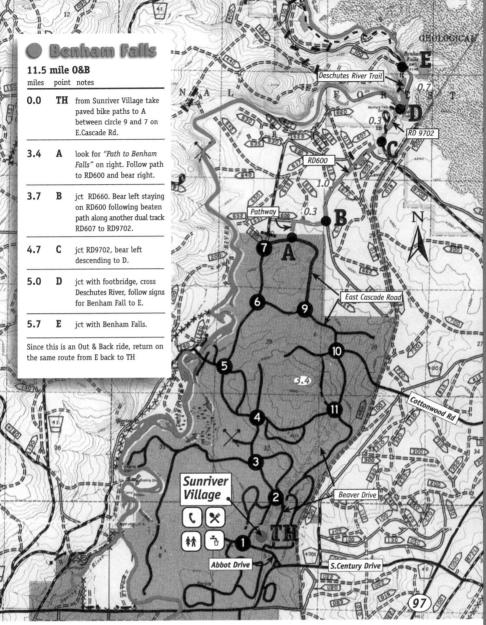

Benham Falls

11.5 mile O&B

miles	point	notes
0.0	TH	from Sunriver Village take paved bike paths to A between circle 9 and 7 on E.Cascade Rd.
3.4	A	look for *"Path to Benham Falls"* on right. Follow path to RD600 and bear right.
3.7	B	jct RD660. Bear left staying on RD600 following beaten path along another dual track RD607 to RD9702.
4.7	C	jct RD9702, bear left descending to D.
5.0	D	jct with footbridge, cross Deschutes River, follow signs for Benham Fall to E.
5.7	E	jct with Benham Falls.

Since this is an Out & Back ride, return on the same route from E back to TH

Slough Camp Loop 🚶🚶 🚴 🐎 17 Mile Loop

Cardinal Landing to Slough Camp Day Use Area and the Deschutes River Trail

● **TERRAIN** 20% singletrack, 50% dual track Forest Service roads, 30% paved bike paths.

■ **FITNESS** More difficult, mean elevation 4200', total gain about 600'.

■ **LENGTH** 17 miles. More difficult to navigate. **SEASON** Spring – Fall. **USE** Moderate.

Getting There ... The Sunriver community is located about 15 miles south of downtown Bend on Hwy97. Heading south from Bend, take a right toward Sunriver off Hwy97 on S. Century Drive, RD40. Follow S. Century Drive about 2.5 miles to Abbot Drive then turn right again, following signs for Sunriver Village. Trail narration begins from the Sunriver Village Mall. Please note vehicle parking is restricted to public areas only within Sunriver.

On the Trail ... From Sunriver Village make your way on the paved bike paths to Cardinal Landing just west of Circle 5. Using a free local map, we managed to find our way on the paved bike paths parallel to Circle 2, 3, and 4 to Circle 5 before crossing the bridge over the Deschutes River at Cardinal Landing. This is a good ride for the more physically fit mountain biker as the total length is fairly long. Reasonable navigation skills are also good to have as there are many Forest Service roads along this ride. We found our way although at times we had to trust our instincts at many road junctions and hope for the best. The bonus parts of this ride are the cruising gradual descent on RD400 down to Slough Camp plus the scenic return to Sunriver on the Deschutes River Trail. — *T.B*

Notes ... Although you won't find many equestrians on the Sunriver bike paths, be aware of guided horseback tours during the summer between Cardinal Landing and Benham Falls on the Forest Service roads. Be sure to slow down and stop when horses are near, then ask for instructions.

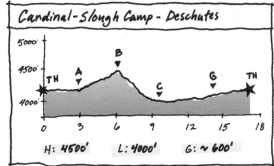

■ Slough Camp Loop

17 mile loop

miles	point	notes
0.0	TH	from Sunriver Village take bike paths to Cardinal Landing at circle 5.
3.0	A	cross Deschutes River, bear left and climb on RD280.
6.0	B	go right on abandoned RD400 over numerous dirt berms, look for powerlines overhead about halfway to C.
9.0	C	jct with RD100, go right on RD100 to Slough Day Use area just ahead on the left. Go left into Slough area.
9.5	D	jct Deschutes River Trail. Follow trail past Benham Falls to F.
11.9	E	jct RD9702 just across footbridge. Follow red cinder RD9702 to RD607. Go right briefly on RD607 then bear left on RD600 to F.
13.2	F	jct with RD660, bear right staying on RD600 to sign and path to G.
13.5	G	take bike paths via Circle 9, 10, 11 back to Sunriver Village at TH.

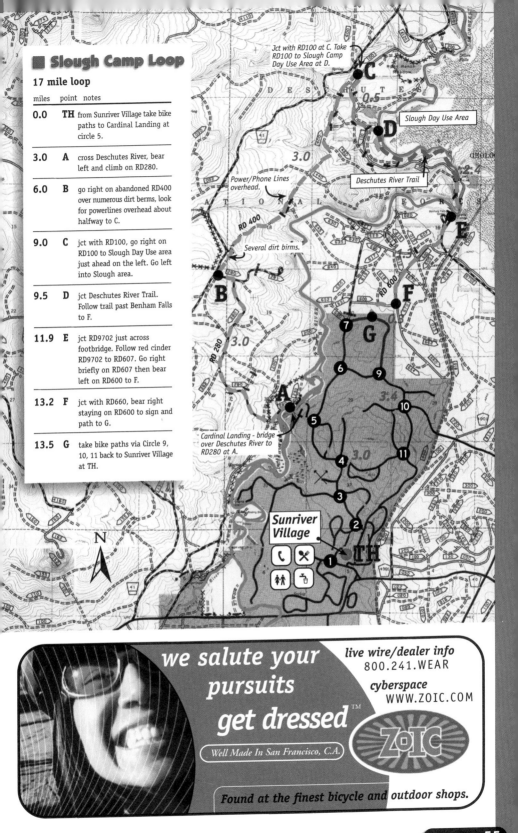

Jct with RD100 at C. Take RD100 to Slough Camp Day Use Area at D.

Slough Day Use Area

Power/Phone Lines overhead.

Deschutes River Trail

Several dirt birms.

Cardinal Landing - bridge over Deschutes River to RD280 at A.

Sunriver Village

N

Benham Butte

🚶 🚴 🐎 **14 Mile Loop**

Cardinal Landing, Benham Butte and Benham Falls Loop

- **TERRAIN** 65% singletrack and abandoned dual track trails, some mild exposure, paved paths within Sunriver to and from the trailhead.
- **FITNESS** More difficult, mean elevation 4200', total gain about 450'.
- **LENGTH** 14 miles. More difficult to navigate. **SEASON** Spring – Fall. **USE** Moderate.

Getting There ... Sunriver is located about 15 miles south of Bend on Hwy97. Take S. Century Drive heading west toward Sunriver off of Hwy97. At Abbot Drive about 2 miles from Hwy 97, go right and follow signs for Sunriver Village. The trail narration begins from Sunriver Village Mall. Please note vehicle parking is restricted to public areas only within Sunriver.

On the Trail ... This is a great trail for a quick and challenging singletrack ride from Sunriver. Using a free Sunriver map, make your way to the Cardinal Landing Bridge just west of Circle 5, where it crosses the Deschutes River. The trail is immediately on cyclist's right once across the bridge. There were obvious signs of horse traffic as we took the trail heading downstream. After following the river a ways the trail climbed up to a rock ledge overlooking Sunriver and the Deschutes River. Once the climb ended we were rewarded with a challenging descent, but be sure to keep an eye on your speed due to horse traffic in the area. At just over 5 miles we were climbing again; this time to the right of a large hill known as Benham Butte. We could hear the Deschutes River below rushing over Benham Falls. Once on the northeast side of Benham Butte there are many trail options, although our notes depict only one option, most lead to the same location. The Deschutes River is not far below where Benham Falls is worthy of a look. Sunriver is a little over two miles farther to the south past Benham Falls. — *KR*

Notes ... When riding in soft conditions lower tire pressure, around 35 psi, can be very helpful. Horse traffic is frequently found on this trail, so please ride with this in mind.

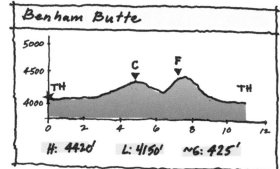

Benham Butte

14 mile Loop

miles	point	notes
0.0	TH	take paved bike paths to Circle 5, cross Cardinal Landing Bridge to A.
2.5	A	take intermittent singletrack and dual track, thru gate climbing to B.
3.7	B	look for singletrack on right, becomes intermittent dual and singletrack trail to C.
5.0	C	cross road, descend to D.
5.6	D	jct with meadow area, follow beaten path left to E.
6.1	E	jct with dual track, right and climbing to F.
7.3	F	Y in road, go left then right beginning to descend toward river to G.
8.3	G	follow beaten path over some whoop-dee-doos to Benham Falls, then follow path to H.
9.0	H	jct RD9702 just after crossing bridge. Follow red cinder RD9702 to dirt RD607 on right which joins RD600 bearing left headed for I.
10.4	I	bear right at I then left on dirt road to J jct E. Cascade Road by Tournament Lane.
10.8	J	follow paved bike paths via Circle 9, 10, 11, and 2 back to Sunriver Village at TH.

Deschutes River Trail

The Deschutes River Trail from Sunriver Village to Meadow Day Use Area

21 Mile O&B

- **TERRAIN** 85% singletrack, 15% dual track, mild exposure, smooth singletrack trail, some seasona dusty conditions, very scenic.
- **FITNESS** More difficult, mean elevation 4000', total gain about 700'.
- **LENGTH** 21 miles. Easier to navigate.   **SEASON** Year Round*.   **USE** Extreme.

*winter weather permitting

Getting There ... The Sunriver community is located about 15 miles south of downtown Bend on Hwy97 and just 18 miles east of Mt. Bachelor. Heading south from Bend, take a right on S. Century Drive, RD40, toward Sunriver off Hwy97. Follow S. Century just over 2 miles to Abbot Drive then turn right again and follow signs for Sunriver Village. Please note vehicle parking is restricted to public areas only within Sunriver. The trail narration begins off of E. Cascade Road between Circle 7 and Circle 9. Use the "Sunriver to Benham Falls" narration (p.52) to find your way to the trailhead.

On the Trail ... The 10 plus miles between Sunriver and the Meadow Picnic Area located at the north end of the trail are extremely popular. This gentle trail follows the scenic Deschutes River as it meanders its way through the Deschutes National Forest on its way to the Columbia River more than 150 miles away. This sect of the Deschutes carves its way through ancient obsidian lava flows and drops off several breathtaking falls. Hikers, bikers, whitewater rafters, fly fishermen, canoers and equestrians are likely to be seen along the trail regardless of the day. Keep in mind the total distance from Sunriver to Meadow Picnic Area and back is more than 20 miles, but since the ride is an "Out & Back" it is easily cut short. Use Slough Day Use Area, Ryan Ranch Meadow or Dillon Falls as potential turn-around points if the full length doesn't fit your schedule. Pac some extra snacks because you'll find lots of scenic overlooks and great spots to kick back, relax and take it all in. — *T.B.*

Notes ... Access to cyclists on this trail is a sensitive issue as the trail is designated for hiking. Ride responsibly, in control, and be sure to yield to all other trail users.

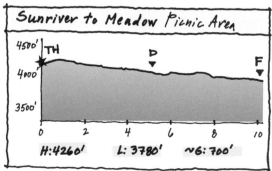

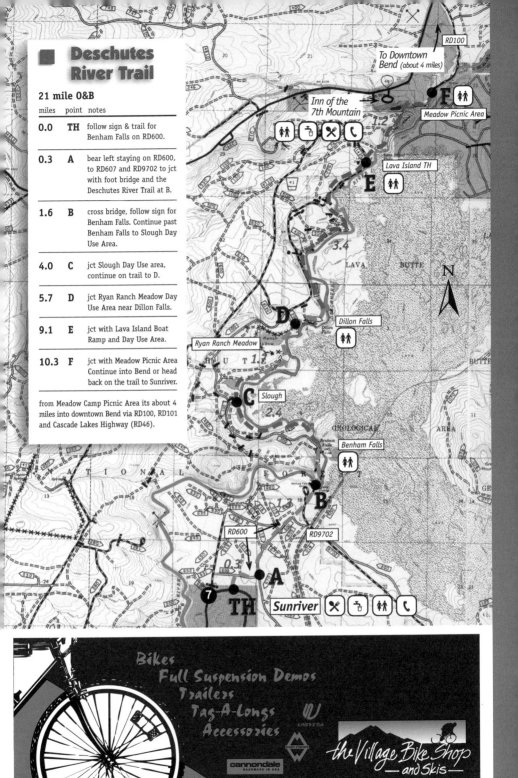

Deschutes River Trail

21 mile O&B

miles	point	notes
0.0	TH	follow sign & trail for Benham Falls on RD600.
0.3	A	bear left staying on RD600, to RD607 and RD9702 to jct with foot bridge and the Deschutes River Trail at B.
1.6	B	cross bridge, follow sign for Benham Falls. Continue past Benham Falls to Slough Day Use Area.
4.0	C	jct Slough Day Use area, continue on trail to D.
5.7	D	jct Ryan Ranch Meadow Day Use Area near Dillon Falls.
9.1	E	jct with Lava Island Boat Ramp and Day Use Area.
10.3	F	jct with Meadow Picnic Area Continue into Bend or head back on the trail to Sunriver.

from Meadow Camp Picnic Area its about 4 miles into downtown Bend via RD100, RD101 and Cascade Lakes Highway (RD46).

To Downtown Bend (about 4 miles)

Inn of the 7th Mountain

Meadow Picnic Area

Lava Island TH

Dillon Falls

Ryan Ranch Meadow

Slough

Benham Falls

Sunriver

RD600

RD9702

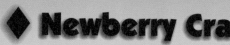

◆ Newberry Crater

🚶🚶 🚲 **20 Mile Loop**

The Rim Trail at Newberry National Volcanic Monument

- **TERRAIN** 85% singletrack, 3 mile dual track climb at start, loose pumice soils in areas, some rocky technical sections, smooth singletrack in others.
- ◆ **FITNESS** Most difficult, mean elevation 6500′, total gain more than 2000′.
- ◆ **LENGTH** 20 miles. More difficult to navigate. **SEASON** Summer – Fall. **USE** Moderate.

Getting There ... 20 miles. It's about 20 miles from Sunriver to the Newberry Crater Visitor Center. From Sunriver take S. Century Drive (RD40) eastbound just over 2 miles to Hwy97 and turn right heading south toward LaPine. Go about 10 miles to RD21 then turn left heading for Paulina Lake Resort. Go anoth er 9 miles or so, to the Newberry Crater Visitor Center on the right about a quarter mile past Paulina Lake Resort. Ride begins here.

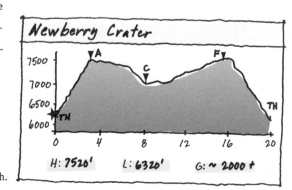

On the Trail ... Oregon's high desert, seven to eight Cascade volcanic peaks, and the crystal clear waters of both Paulina Lake and East Lake are wa ing. The "Rim Trail" of this ancient volcanic crater challenges cyclists with its loose pumice soils and rolling terrain, not to mention the views continually drawing your attention. The Visitor Center serves as a good sta ing place as both drinking water and restrooms are near. We began our ride on RD21 for a short bit then climbed on RD500 to the singletrack. After this warm-up, you'll be ready to test your skills on the singletrac Be sure to pace yourself as there is quite a bit of climbing during this 20 mile ride. Once you make your way around the crater to the north side, the view into the crater below can't be beat. From here the trail descend about 1200 vertical feet back down to the shore by Lake Paulina Lodge. We then fol lowed RD21 back to the Visitor Center fin ishing this long ride. — *T.B.*

Notes ... Several other shorter trail options exists descending down to RD21 from TR57, offering less than ◆ riding conditions and an abbreviated total length.

Newberry Crater

7500 — ▼A   C ▼   F ▼
7000
6500 — ▼TH
6000 —

0   4   8   12   16   20

H: 7520′   L: 6320′   G: ~ 2000 +

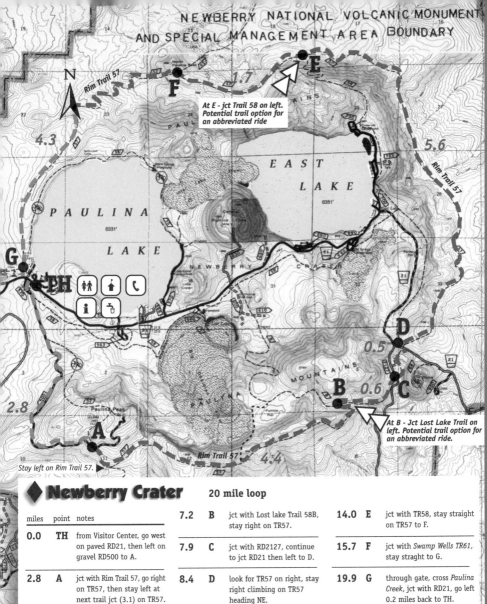

At E - jct Trail 58 on left. Potential trail option for an abbreviated ride

At B - Jct Lost Lake Trail on left. Potential trail option for an abbreviated ride.

Stay left on Rim Trail 57.

◆ Newberry Crater   20 mile loop

miles	point	notes
0.0	TH	from Visitor Center, go west on paved RD21, then left on gravel RD500 to A.
2.8	A	jct with Rim Trail 57, go right on TR57, then stay left at next trail jct (3.1) on TR57.
7.2	B	jct with Lost lake Trail 58B, stay right on TR57.
7.9	C	jct with RD2127, continue to jct RD21 then left to D.
8.4	D	look for TR57 on right, stay right climbing on TR57 heading NE.
14.0	E	jct with TR58, stay straight on TR57 to F.
15.7	F	jct with Swamp Wells TR61, stay straght to G.
19.9	G	through gate, cross Paulina Creek, jct with RD21, go left 0.2 miles back to TH.

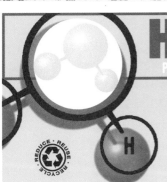

Know the Rules of the Trail...

Ride On Open Trails Only.
Riding closed trails makes it difficult for responsible cyclists and groups like COTA to convince officials that mountain bikers are responsible outdoor enthusiasts.

Leave No Trace.
Tread lightly. Don't skid your tires. Pack out at least as much as you pack in.

Control You Bike At All Times.
Be alert. Practice low impact, safe cycling techniques that maximize control and minimize impact

Plan Your Ride.
Be self sufficient. Know your equipment, your ability and the area you are riding. Plan accordingly. Bring other maps.

Never Spook Animals.
Slow down and use special care around horses, dogs and other animals. Ask horseback riders and dog owners the best way to ensure a safe pass.

Always Wear A Helmet.
Wear protective gear including a helmet and eye protection. Protective gear can save your life if you fall.

Respect The Land.
Don't skid or cut corners. Stay on established trails and don't make new ones.

What Else?
Ride responsibly. Be friendly and go out of your way to be courteous. Educate your friends and fellow cyclists on these rules. Volunteer. Have fun. Be safe.

I·M·B·A

COTA and The Singletrack Anthology encourage all riders to follow the rules of the International Mountain Biking Association to ensure fun and a safe time for all trail users.

Check Locally.

Trail conditions vary from season to season. Trails can be closed due to sensitive wildlife habitat or fire danger. Trails may also be unmaintained due to time of season, severity of weather and acts of God. Check with your local authority for the most current information.

Bend/Fort Rock Ranger District	541/388-5664
Bend Metro Parks and Rec	541/389-7275
Sisters Ranger District	541/549-2111
McKenzie River Ranger District	541/822-3381
Oak Ridge Ranger District	541/782-2283
Willamette National Forest	541/465-6521

Best Downhills – Bachelor to Bend, McKenzie River Trail, Windigo-Brad's Trail.
Choice Singletrack – North Fork-Flagline, Swede Ridge-Tumalo Falls.
Great Beginner Rides – Swampy Lakes Loop, Benham Falls, Suttle Lake.
Technical Rides – Edison to Lava Lake, Newberry Crater, Cache Mountain.

About the Authors.

Kent Reynolds is a partner in Outside Sales, a company representing a variety of products in the cycling, outdoor and winter recreation industries. Kent spends a great deal of his time on the road visiting local shops and selling product. When home, he's cruising the trails either on a mountain bike or motorcycle. Kent resides in Portland, Oregon with Jenifer and his basset hound Lucy.

Tyler Barnes is a graphic designer who runs a publishing and design business in Hood River, Oregon. While print and web projects consume much of his time, he also teaches both alpine and telemark skiing as well as snowboarding at Mt. Hood Meadows Ski Resort during the winter. In the summer months you're likely to catch him cranking on the trails and announcing races in The Gorge and on Mt. Hood.

A collection of singletrack mountain bike trails based out of Hood River, Oregon.

Tyler Barnes & Kent Reynolds

Get the Hood River - Mt. Hood Book too!

The Singletrack Anthology Series.

The Singletrack Anthology Series is a collection of mountain bike guidebooks. The full color presentation offers information about trail conditions, how to get to trailheads and promotes local businesses who embrace mountain biking in their communities. Look for the Anthology in the area near you.

The Singletrack Anthology – Willamette Valley. Covering areas within Portland, Salem and Eugene - available in 1999.

The Singletrack Anthology – Hood River. Covers area of Mt. Hood, The Gorge and Mt. Adams - first published May 1996.

www.SingletrackAnthology.com

Don't forget to register your book at our website providing you with FREE on-line updates, bonus rides, and information on rides in other areas and other Singletrack Anthology editions.